Marking Our Past

Marking Our Past

WEST VIRGINIA'S HISTORICAL HIGHWAY MARKERS

Published by the
State of West Virginia
West Virginia Division of Culture and History
Charleston, West Virginia 25305

*Proceeds from the sale of this publication benefit the
West Virginia State Historical Highway Marker Program.*

ISBN 0-9717372-0-7

West Virginia Division of Culture and History, The Cultural Center,
    1900 Kanawha Boulevard, East, Charleston, West Virginia 25305-0300
Printed in the United States of America

Design by Leslie Chincheck
Cover photo: West Virginia State Capitol, Charleston, by Ed Hicks
Back cover: Morgan's Chapel, Bunker Hill, by Rick Lee

Published by the
STATE OF WEST VIRGINIA

Bob Wise
Governor

Kay Goodwin
Secretary of Education and the Arts

Nancy P. Herholdt
Commissioner of Culture and History

Fredrick H. Armstrong
Director of Archives and History

Joe Geiger
Project Manager/Editor

ACKNOWLEDGMENTS

Stan Bumgardner and Chris Kreiser
Initial Project Coordinators

Debra Basham, Mary Johnson, Terry Lowry, Cathy Miller,
Sharon Newhouse, Deborah Tucker, Nancy Waggoner
Editorial Assistants

Greg Clark and Ed Hicks
Photographic Assistants

Hunter Armentrout, Fredrick Armstrong, Debra Basham, Jeannie Bess,
Pat Bonar, Margaret Brennan, Stan Bumgardner, Richard Fauss,
Alan Freeman, Joe Geiger, Ruby Greathouse, Kim Johnson,
Katherine Jourdan, Chris Kreiser, Emily Neff, Zane Perry, Ron Ripley,
Ann Sandor, Bill Theriault, Nancy Waggoner, Don Wood
Marker Surveyors

Marker survey and publication funded in part from the
Federal Highway Administration's Transportation Enhancement Program
administered by the
West Virginia Department of Transportation, Division of Highways

Fred VanKirk, P.E., Secretary/Commissioner of Highways

I am pleased to present this latest edition of the guide to West Virginia's historical highway markers. Whether you are a West Virginian or a visitor to our fine state, I know you will find much to interest you in these pages.

Our beautiful state, though small in size, has a disproportionately rich history. Within West Virginia, one can discover many stories which have shaped our nation–the exploration and settlement of the frontier, the French and Indian War, and the Civil War and statehood. We also enjoy a wealth of natural resources and beautiful natural attractions, as well as an abundant legacy of native sons and daughters whose lives have inspired us all. These stories and more are featured in the hundreds of highway markers found along thoroughfares throughout our 55 counties.

I hope the marker inscriptions and photographs in this publication will encourage you to visit many of the places highlighted. Happy exploring!

Bob Wise
Governor

Our agency is indeed proud to be involved with the West Virginia State Historical Highway Marker Program. First implemented more than 75 years ago, the marker program remains one of the most popular and visible projects with which we are charged.

Our mission to identify, preserve, protect, promote and present West Virginia's heritage is embodied in the historical highway markers. Designed to attract travelers' attention to points of interest, these distinct roadside signs provide information about historic events and places that might otherwise be overlooked in today's busy world.

Thank you to the many private citizens who have helped underwrite the cost of markers and to those who assist in the upkeep and preservation of the signs. Thanks also to our partner, the West Virginia Department of Transportation, Division of Highways, for its continuing support of these efforts. Without cooperation from the private and public sector, we would not be able to continue this important program.

Nancy P. Herholdt
Commissioner of Culture and History
State Historic Preservation Officer

PREFACE

A great source of pride in West Virginia's fascinating state and local history, the Mountain State's historical highway markers have attracted the interest and attention of young and old for some 65 years. Whether it is the Boy Scout who retrieved a lost marker from a stream bed and refurbished it for re-installation, or the nationwide family association whose members made contributions to sponsor a sign designating the home place of their progenitor, people from all walks of life regard these cast aluminum plaques as a vital personal and visual connection to the state's past.

Local citizens and civic groups often adopt markers, providing maintenance and security. This involvement and vigilance ensure these brief accounts of our state's exciting history will be available for future generations. The signs have served as student research projects and as service projects, where young citizens have cleaned and restored them. Travelers even plan driving tours based upon the markers' locations and topics. *Marking Our Past: West Virginia's Historical Highway Markers* addresses all these interests by making the state's prehistoric, historic, scenic and geological highway marker inscriptions and locations available in a readily accessible format for enjoyment by the motoring or armchair traveler.

This book features nearly 1,000 West Virginia historical highway markers erected since the first sign was installed in 1937. Early markers produced under the auspices of county historical and patriotic groups also are included.

Arranged alphabetically by county, markers with a different inscription on each side are listed with a double title. Asterisks (*) denote markers missing at the time of the most recent survey. New or replacement markers approved by the West Virginia Archives and History Commission but not erected at the time this publication went to press are listed on page 1. These pending markers will be included in future editions of the book and will be posted on the Division's website when they are erected.

As you read the marker text, you will notice that space limitations on the signs often necessitated awkward phrasing and abbreviations. Also keep in mind that inscriptions for many of these markers were written more than 60 years ago; therefore, some of the wording is obsolete (i.e., the term "savages" used to refer to Native Americans) and is not considered acceptable language by today's standards. These outmoded markers are being updated as funding becomes available.

Readers are encouraged to visit the many sites commemorated by these official West Virginia historical highway markers. For more information about the highway marker program, or to report missing signs or discrepancies in the inscriptions, please contact the Archives and History Section, West Virginia Division of Culture and History, The Cultural Center, 1900 Kanawha Boulevard, East, Charleston, WV 25305-0300. Call (304) 558-0230 or visit the agency's website at www.wvculture.org/history/.

Fredrick H. Armstrong, Director of Archives and History
West Virginia Division of Culture and History

"LOST COLONY"

In 1772, Washington patented 10,990 acres along the Great Kanawha River. In 1775, he had James Cleveland and William Stevens lead colonist there. Land was cleared; orchards planted; houses built. But when war ended, colony was gone.

School children admiring a West Virginia historic highway marker along U.S. Route 35 in Mason County, circa 1960.

HISTORY OF THE MARKER PROGRAM

West Virginia's historical highway marker program was initiated in 1934 during the administration of Governor Herman Guy Kump as a means of promoting interest in the state's history. According to the late Dr. Roy Bird Cook, an avocational historian and long-time member of the Commission on Historic and Scenic Highway Markers, the markers were intended to tell the story of West Virginia and its history as concisely as possible and were placed close to the road to be most visible to travelers.

County workers across the state initially compiled information about 5,000 potential marker sites. Of these, 440 markers were selected by the Commission on Historic and Scenic Highway Markers, and inscriptions were written and submitted for public comment. Topics of the original markers included brief state and county histories; county seats, towns and communities; colonial, Revolutionary and Civil War activities; early settlements and settlers; prominent personalities; and scenic attractions.

Significant federal funding from the New Deal Federal Emergency Relief Administration, as well as state support from the State Road Commission and the Commission on Historic and Scenic Highway Markers, financed the placement of 440 markers along highways in 1937. The original markers–including the first marker placed in Charleston on Capitol Street in April 1937–were made by Michaels Art Bronze of cast aluminum. The standard design adopted by the commission is still in use today: approximately 42 inches wide by 30 inches high with a 9-inch circular West Virginia state seal centered on top. Each marker cost $41. The following year, the State Road Commission funded the printing of 50,000 copies of the first marker book, *West Virginia Historic and Scenic Highway Markers*. The 250-page, glove-box-size publication presented the marker titles, inscriptions and locations, complete with maps providing regional tours for travelers.

With the end of the Depression-era federal programs and the outbreak of World War II, interest in the marker program waned. Over the next two decades only a few markers were installed, mostly at various state institutions and facilities. The Civil War and West Virginia state centennials in the 1960s generated a resurgence of interest in state and local history. The newly created West Virginia Historic Commission collaborated with the West Virginia Department of Archives and History to sponsor an inventory of markers, and proceeded to replace both missing and damaged markers and to erect new markers. Over the course of four years, more than 400 markers were installed. Nearly 300 designated new sites, many recognizing Civil War topics and geological formations. This second set of markers, made on the same design as the original and using the same traditional sand-mold casting, were manufactured by Sewah Studios at a cost of $250 each. This intensive activity concluded with the 1967 publication of *West Virginia Highway Markers* by the West Virginia Historic Commission under the auspices of the Department of Archives and History.

Today, the West Virginia State Historical Highway Marker Program is overseen by the West Virginia Division of Culture and History, Archives and

History Section, and the West Virginia Archives and History Commission. It is a collaboration with the West Virginia Department of Transportation, Division of Highways, which installs the markers on the state right-of-way. Replacement and new-marker purchases have continued over the past 30 years, but as costs have increased and state funding allocations have declined, the program has been unable to fully address public interest or maintenance needs.

Since 1985, new markers, which now cost approximately $1,500 each, have been financed primarily through private donations, but the absence of funding for maintenance and for replacement of missing, outdated or damaged markers continues to be a problem. To address these growing needs, the Division of Culture and History submitted a request in the 1990s for funding through the Federal Highway Administration to survey existing markers, identify replacement needs and publish a new guide. With the support of then-Division of Culture and History commissioner William M. Drennen Jr., Division of Highways commissioner Fred VanKirk and Governor Gaston Caperton, the grant was awarded.

This most recent survey found nearly one-third of the markers were either missing or in need of repair. As a result, the Division of Culture and History obtained funding from the West Virginia Celebration 2000 initiative to replace markers with outdated inscriptions and to install new markers focusing on ethnic and women's history, industrial and labor history, and African-American history. These, as well as a number of privately funded markers, were pending manufacture and installation when this publication was prepared in late 2001.

Fredrick H. Armstrong

TABLE OF CONTENTS

PENDING MARKERS
As of January 2002, these new and replacement markers were pending manufacture and placement.

*Battle of Blair Mountain .... Logan
*Berkeley Springs Baths ...... Morgan
Bethel United
   Methodist Church .... Nicholas
Benedum Civic Center .... Harrison
*Border Heroine .... Monongalia
Brickyard Bend .... Hancock
*Bulltown/Bulltown Battle . Braxton
Camp Glass .... Cabell
Carter G. Woodson .... Cabell
*Cass .... Pocahontas
Christopher H. Payne .... Fayette
Civil War Camp/Mike Foster
   C.S.A. Sharpshooter .... Summers
Coal River
   Covered Bridge .... Kanawha
*Cook's Fort .... Monroe
*Denmar State Hospital...Pocahontas
Dick Pointer .... Greenbrier
Dr. W.J. Humphreys/
   Gap Mills .... Monroe
Escape to Freedom/
   Women of Courage .... Wood
First Nicholas
   County Court .... Nicholas
First Public School............... Nicholas
First State Capitol Building ...... Ohio
*Hamlin .... Lincoln
*Harpers Ferry/
   John Brown's Fort .... Jefferson
J.R. Clifford .... Berkeley
John Hinton .... Summers
Johnsontown .... Jefferson
Julia Augusta Robertson Pierpont/
   Decoration Day .... Marion
Keslers Cross Lanes .... Nicholas
Knights of Labor
   Headquarters .... Fayette

Knights of Labor
   Headquarters .... Wetzel
*Lakin State Hospital .... Mason
Libby-Owens-Ford Glass/Union Glass
   and Ceramic Workers .... Kanawha
*Lorentz................................. Upshur
Martin Robinson Delany ... Jefferson
Mason Star Lodge #1/
   Old Stone House .... Jefferson
*Mt. De Chantal .... Ohio
Nallen/Wilderness Lumber
   Company .... Fayette
Nellis/Armco Coal .... Boone
Nestorville Spring................ Barbour
*New Martinsville .... Wetzel
Old Town .... Hancock
Owens-Illinois Bottle Plant . Marion
Pence Springs Resort/
   Women's Prison .... Summers
Pinoak Fountain .... Hampshire
Pioneer School
   (First County School) ...... Summers
*Seneca Rocks .... Pendleton
*Spencer State Hospital .... Roane
*Spruce Knob .... Pendleton
Stanaford .... Raleigh
Sumner School/
   Robert W. Simmons .... Wood
The Labor Star .... Cabell
*Vincent Williams .... Grant
Welch Community Hospital/
   Miners' Hospital .... McDowell
West Va. Colored
   Children's Home .... Cabell
Wheeling Hospital .... Ohio
World War I Memorial .... McDowell

*Denotes replacement markers

1

WEST VIRGINIA

"The Mountain State"—western part of the Commonwealth of Virginia until June 20, 1863. Settled by the Germans and Scotch-Irish. It became a line of defense between the English and French during the French and Indian War, 1754-1763.

*WV 45	Berkeley-Virginia border
*US 11	Berkeley-Virginia border
WV 27	Brooke-Pennsylvania border
*WV 67	Brooke-Pennsylvania border
*US 52 and 6th Street, Huntington	Cabell-Ohio border
*US 50	Hampshire-Virginia border
WV 259	Hampshire-Virginia border
*WV 55	Hardy-Virginia border
*WV 480	Jefferson-Maryland border
WV 891	Marshall-Pennsylvania border
*US 33	Mason-Ohio border
WV 2 (Mason County Courthouse)	Mason-Ohio border
*WV 16	McDowell-Virginia border
WV 83	McDowell-Virginia border
*WV 102	Mercer-Virginia border
*US 460	Mercer-Virginia border
*WV 28	Mineral-Maryland border
*US 220	Mineral-Maryland border
*US 52	Mingo-Kentucky border
*US 119	Mingo-Kentucky border
*US 19	Monongalia-Pennsylvania border
US 119	Monongalia-Pennsylvania border
*WV 311/WV 3	Monroe-Virginia border
*US 219	Monroe-Virginia border
*US 522	Morgan-Maryland border
*US 522	Morgan-Virginia border
*US 33	Pendleton-Virginia border
US 220	Pendleton-Virginia border
US 250	Pocahontas-Virginia border
WV 39	Pocahontas-Virginia border
US 60	Wayne-Kentucky border
*WV 2	Wetzel-Ohio border
*WV 69	Wetzel-Pennsylvania border
WV 14/WV 68	Wood-Ohio border

KENTUCKY

Named for the Kentucky River, bearing an Indian name. Called "Dark and Bloody Ground." Explored by Daniel Boone, 1769. Settled at Harrodsburg, 1774. It became a Virginia county in 1776 and a state in the Union in 1792.

WV 49 .... Mingo-Kentucky border
*WV 37 .... Wayne-Kentucky border
*US 52 .... West Virginia (Mingo)-Kentucky border
US 119 .... West Virginia (Mingo)-Kentucky border
US 60 .... West Virginia (Wayne)-Kentucky border

MARYLAND

Named for Queen Henrietta Maria, the wife of Charles I, who gave a royal charter to Cecil Calvert, second Lord Baltimore, 1632. First settled at Saint Mary's City in 1634. It is one of the thirteen original colonies.

*US 11 .... Berkeley-Maryland border
*US 50 .... Grant-Maryland border
US 340 .... Jefferson-Maryland border
*WV 46 .... Mineral-Maryland border
*WV 42 .... Mineral-Maryland border
*WV 9 .... Morgan-Maryland border
US 50 .... Preston-Maryland border
US 219 .... Preston-Maryland border
*WV 7 .... Preston-Maryland border
*WV 480 .... West Virginia (Jefferson)-Maryland border
*WV 28 .... West Virginia (Mineral)-Maryland border
*US 220 .... West Virginia (Mineral)-Maryland border
*US 522 .... West Virginia (Morgan)-Maryland border

OHIO

Named for the river, called by the Iroquois the "Beautiful River." Visited by LaSalle in 1669-1670. Once part of the Northwest Territory. Settled at Marietta, 1788. Admitted to the Union, 1803. Home of 8 United States Presidents.

US 22 .... Brooke-Ohio border
First Street, Weirton .... Hancock-Ohio border
US 40/US 250, Wheeling Island .... Ohio County-Ohio border
WV 2 .... Pleasants-Ohio border
US 50 .... Wood-Ohio border
*WV 14, Williamstown .... Wood-Ohio border
*US 52 and 6th Street, Huntington .... West Virginia
(Cabell)-Ohio border
Off WV 2, (Mason County Courthouse) .... West Virginia
(Mason)-Ohio border
*US 33 .... West Virginia (Mason)-Ohio border
*WV 2 .... West Virginia (Wetzel)-Ohio border
Off WV 14/WV 68, Parkersburg Memorial Bridge ..... West Virginia
(Wood)-Ohio border

PENNSYLVANIA

Named for William Penn to whom it was granted in 1681 by Charles II. In 1682, Penn made his first settlement at Philadelphia. Earlier settlements had been made by the Swedes in 1638. It was one of the thirteen original colonies.

County Route 22/1 .... Hancock-Pennsylvania border
*US 30 .... Hancock-Pennsylvania border
US 40 .... Ohio-Pennsylvania border
*WV 26 .... Preston-Pennsylvania border
*WV 67 .... West Virginia (Brooke)-Pennsylvania border
WV 27 .... West Virginia (Brooke)-Pennsylvania border
WV 891 .... West Virginia (Marshall)-Pennsylvania border
*US 19 .... West Virginia (Monongalia)-Pennsylvania border
US 119 .... West Virginia (Monongalia)-Pennsylvania border
*WV 69 .... West Virginia (Wetzel)-Pennsylvania border

VIRGINIA

Named for Queen Elizabeth, the Virgin Queen of England. Site of the first permanent English settlement in America, 1607. One of the 13 original colonies. The Old Dominion is the birthplace of eight United States Presidents.

*US 60 .... Greenbrier-Virginia border
*WV 127 .... Hampshire-Virginia border
*County Route 59 (Lower Cove Run Road) ... Hardy-Virginia border
WV 259 .... Hardy-Virginia border
WV 9 .... Jefferson-Virginia border
US 340 .... Jefferson-Virginia border
*US 52 .... Mercer-Virginia border
*US 19 .... Mercer-Virginia border
*WV 84 .... Pocahontas-Virginia border
*US 11 .... West Virginia (Berkeley)-Virginia border
*US 45 .... West Virginia (Berkeley)-Virginia border
*US 50 .... West Virginia (Hampshire)-Virginia border
WV 259 .... West Virginia (Hampshire)-Virginia border
*WV 55 .... West Virginia (Hardy)-Virginia border
*WV 16 .... West Virginia (McDowell)-Virginia border
WV 83 .... West Virginia (McDowell)-Virginia border
*US 460 .... West Virginia (Mercer)-Virginia border
*WV 102 .... West Virginia (Mercer)-Virginia border
*WV 311/WV 3 .... West Virginia (Monroe)-Virginia border
*US 219 .... West Virginia (Monroe)-Virginia border
*US 522 .... West Virginia (Morgan)-Virginia border
US 220 .... West Virginia (Pendleton)-Virginia border
US 33 .... West Virginia (Pendleton)-Virginia border
WV 39 .... West Virginia (Pocahontas)-Virginia border
US 250 .... West Virginia (Pocahontas)-Virginia border

WEST VIRGINIA COUNTIES AND SURROUNDING STATES

BARBOUR COUNTY

Formed from Harrison, Lewis and Randolph in 1843. It is named for Philip Pendleton Barbour, distinguished Virginia jurist. The scene of opening hostilities on land between the armies of the North and the South in 1861.

*WV 20, Barbour-Harrison border; WV 57, Barbour-Harrison border; WV 92, Barbour-Preston border; US 250, Barbour-Randolph border; US 119 and US 250, Barbour-Taylor border; WV 76, Barbour-Taylor border; WV 38, Barbour-Tucker border; WV 20, Barbour-Upshur border; *US 119, Barbour-Upshur border*

VALLEY FURNACE

Iron ore was discovered here, 1835, by John Johnson. The Old Iron Furnace, built, 1848, was operated for six years by C.W. Bryant and Isaac Marsh. In 1850, a steam engine replaced the water power used to run fan air blast. Charcoal was fuel used. About 9,000 pounds of iron were produced daily. The iron was hauled by mule team 50 miles to the Monongahela River near Fairmont for shipment by boat to down-river markets.

WV 38, Valley Furnace Roadside Rest Area, 3 miles east of junction with WV 92

CAMP LAUREL HILL

Fortified camp occupied by Confederates under Brig. Gen. Robert S. Garnett, June 16-July 12, 1861. The scene of sharp skirmishes July 7-11. Garnett retreated early in the morning of July 12 after the Rich Mountain defeat.

County Route 15, 1.9 miles east of junction with US 250/WV 92, Belington

LAUREL HILL

Battle of Laurel Hill, July 8, 1861, between Confederates and McClellan's army, followed by actions at Rich Mountain and Corrick's Ford, gave Federals control of State and established communication lines to the West. Fine view from peak.

County Route 15, 2.1 miles east of US 250/ WV 92 at Belington

CAMP BELINGTON

Union troops under Brigadier General T.A. Morris advanced from Philippi on July 7, 1861 and established a fortified camp near this site. Battle of Belington took place July 7-11. Confederates were two miles to east at Laurel Hill.

County Route 15 (Watkins Street), at junction with US 250/WV 92 (Crim Avenue), Belington

MEADOWVILLE

Meadowville, on the site of an Indian fort built in 1784, is a few miles north. New Jersey colonists settled there before 1800, and tavern, mills, and stores made it a trading center of the Tygarts Valley for a hundred years.

WV 92, 0.1 miles north of US 250, Belington

HENRY EVERETT ENGLE
Approximately 1/4 mile west is the birthplace of Henry Everett Engle, the author and composer of original chorus and music for the Rev. David King's poem, "The West Virginia Hills," in 1885. He was born in 1849, died in 1933.

US 119, 2 miles south of junction with WV 57

BIRTHPLACE—W.D. ZINN
One mile east is Woodbine Farm, birthplace of W.D. Zinn, noted farmer, writer and lecturer. He contributed much to scientific farming in this and adjoining states. "The Story of Woodbine Farm" is an autobiography of his work.

US 119/US 250, 0.5 miles north of US 119/US 250 split, Dumont Park, Philippi

IDA L. REED
Northeast, 3 1/2 miles, is the birthplace of Ida L. Reed, born November 30, 1865. She became famous for her religious writings, chiefly cantatas, poems and hymns, of which she wrote over 2000. Her hymns have been used in the services of eleven denominations in America. Many have been translated into foreign languages. Her most noted is "I Belong to the King". Miss Reed died July 8, 1951, and is buried here.

US 119, at junction with County Route 6 (Arden Road), 2.7 miles south of the Taylor County border

HISTORIC CHRISLIP HOLLOW
One mile north of this site is the graveyard of one of West Virginia's pioneer families. Emigrating from Germany in 1765 and Pennsylvania ca. 1782, Revolutionary War Patriot Jacob Christlieb (Chrislip) came to this region with wife, Nancy Singer and reared 7 sons and 7 daughters.

WV 57, at junction with County Route 57/8, Elk City

THE COVERED BRIDGE
The Philippi Covered Bridge across Tygart Valley River was built in 1852 by Lemuel Chenoweth of Beverly. Made of wood, with the exception of the iron bolts used to hold the segments together, it is an example of the best in covered bridge architecture and design. It was used by armies of the North and South in the Civil War. In 1934 the bridge was strengthened to permit modern traffic and is today a part of U.S. 250.

US 250, 0.1 miles west of junction with US 119, Philippi

FIRST LAND BATTLE

First land battle between the North and South here, June 3, 1861. Confederates under Col. Porterfield were dislodged by Federal troops from Gen. McClellan's army under Col. Kelley. The old covered bridge here was used by both armies.

US 119/US 250, 0.5 miles north of US 119/US 250 split, Dumont Park, Philippi

PHILIPPI

Originally called Anglin's Ford for William Anglin but later named Booth's Ferry for Daniel Booth. Near by in 1780, Richard, Cottrill, and Charity Talbott settled. Philippi was named for Judge Philip Pendleton Barbour.

US 250 (Court Street), at junction with North Main Street, Philippi

HISTORIC CAMPBELL SCHOOL/ HISTORIC CAMPBELL SCHOOL

After the Civil War, Barbour County residents built this one-room school house near Volga, 8 miles SW. As one of the county's first free schools, it was the center of education for hundreds of children, providing instruction for primary through eighth grade, until it closed in 1963. In 1992, the restored school was moved to Alderson-Broaddus College campus to insure its preservation.

Noted alumni, Arch Hall, M.D., who performed 1st open-heart surgery in U.S. & Helen Reger, 1976 West Virginia Teacher of the Year were educated in this one-room schoolhouse. Elza and Nola Wilson restored and gave school to Alderson-Broaddus.

Broaddus Road, Alderson-Broaddus campus, Philippi

"The Battle of Philippi" as sketched in the July 6, 1861, issue of Harper's Weekly.

BERKELEY COUNTY

Formed from Frederick in 1772. Named for Norborne Berkeley, Baron Botetourt, governor of Virginia, 1768-1770. Home of many leaders in the Revolution. As early as 1774, George Washington had orchards planted here.

*WV 9, Berkeley-Jefferson border; *WV 45, Berkeley-Jefferson border; WV 51, Berkeley-Jefferson border; WV 9, Berkeley-Morgan border; *US 11, Berkeley-Maryland border*

FORT EVANS

Fort Evans, built here, 1755, was attacked by Indians, 1756. The men were absent but Polly Evans, whose husband, John, had built the fort, led the women in its defense. The Big Spring here was noted camping ground of both armies, 1861-1865.

*US 11, south of Martinsburg

VETERANS ADMINISTRATION CENTER

Established as the Newton D. Baker General Hospital, U.S. Army. Named for Newton D. Baker, native of Martinsburg and Secretary of War, World War I. Opened for patients in 1944. It became Veterans Administration Center in 1946.

WV 9, 4.5 miles south of Martinsburg

VAN METRE FORD BRIDGE

Named for the property owners this stone bridge built in 1832 across Opequon Creek was major improvement for travellers on Warm Springs Road connecting Alexandria and Bath, Va., site of famous mineral waters. The Berkeley County Court established a commission to study and contract for construction of bridge. Silas Harry erected at local expense 165 foot bridge at reported cost of $3,700.

County Route 36 (Needy Road), 2 miles east of Martinsburg

The historic Van Metre Ford Bridge, located near Martinsburg, was built in 1832.

Revolutionary War hero Adam Stephen began construction of his home in Martinsburg in 1772. Today the house is open as a museum.

SWAN POND MANOR

1.5 miles north is Swan Pond Manor, a 2,000 acre retreat set aside in 1745 for use of Thomas Lord Fairfax, once the proprietor of the Northern Neck of Virginia who established an estate at Greenway Court, Frederick County in 1738. So named because wild swans inhabited site. Conveyed in 1775 to John Lewis and in 1801 to Dr. Edward O. Williams who built present manor house circa 1810.

WV 45 and County Route 45/2, 4 miles east of Martinsburg

TUSCARORA CHURCH

Tuscarora Presbyterian Church, which was built before 1745 by Scotch-Irish Presbyterians. Rev. Hugh Vance, first pastor, is buried here. During Indian days, worshipers hung their guns on pegs in the walls while they sang and prayed.

County Route 15 (Tuscarora Pike), approximately 0.5 miles west of I-81 (Exit 13)

GEN. ADAM STEPHEN

Here was home of General Adam Stephen, founder of Martinsburg and county's first sheriff. Famous as fighter in French and Indian War, and as major-general in the American Revolutionary War.

309 East John Street, Martinsburg

RAILROAD STRIKE OF 1877/ ROUNDHOUSES AND SHOPS

On July 16, 1877, workers of the Baltimore and Ohio Railroad went on strike and closed this railroad yard

11

to protest a cut in wages. Their action sparked the largest nationwide strike the country had seen. Extensive damage was done to company property at Pittsburgh, Baltimore and Wheeling, and over 50 workers were killed before the strike was crushed. Federal troops were used for the first time in a labor dispute. As the country's first general strike, it focused national attention on labor's grievances and made workers aware of the power of collective action.

The B&O Railroad reached Martinsburg in 1842, and by 1849, a roundhouse and shops were built. These first buildings were burned by Confederate troops in 1862. The present west roundhouse and the two shops were built in 1866. The east roundhouse was built in 1872. These buildings represent one of the last remaining examples of American industrial railroad architecture still intact and in use. These structures serve as important reminders of the status of the railroad in the mid-19th century and the role it played in the economic development of Martinsburg, the county, and the state.

East Martin Street and Roundhouse Drive at Caperton Station, Martinsburg

MARTINSBURG/ BERKELEY RIFLEMEN
Established, 1778, by General Adam Stephen. Named for Col. Thomas Martin, nephew of Lord Fairfax. Home of Admiral C.K. Stribling and

Admiral Charles Boarman. In Jackson's raid, 1861, captured B&O locomotives were drawn by horses to Winchester.

The Berkeley Riflemen from Eastern Panhandle counties, under Capt. Hugh Stephenson, were first southern troops to join Washington in 1775 at Boston. In a "bee line" from Morgan's Spring, they marched 600 miles in 26 days.

300 West King Street, at old Federal Building, Martinsburg

MARTINSBURG
Founded, 1778, by Gen. Adam Stephen. Named for Thomas Martin, nephew of Lord Fairfax. Home of Admirals Charles Boarman and C.K. Stribling. Locomotives seized here, 1861, in Jackson's raid were drawn by horses to Winchester, Va.

Junction of North Queen Street and Eagle Schoolhouse Road, Martinsburg

BOYDVILLE
Built, 1812, by Elisha Boyd, general in the War of 1812, on land bought from Gen. Adam Stephen. Mansion noted for its fine workmanship. Home of his son-in-law, Charles J. Faulkner, Minister to France, and his grandson, U.S. Senator Faulkner.

600 block of South Queen Street, Martinsburg

FORT NEALLY
During the French and Indian War, Fort Neally was captured and its garrison massacred, Sept. 17, 1756.

Many settlers in the vicinity also were killed. Among captives was Isabella Stockton, later wife of Col. William McCleery, Morgantown.

US 11, 2 miles north of Martinsburg

WATKINS FERRY

By act of the Virginia House of Burgesses 1744, a ferry was established extending from the mouth of Canagochego Creek in Maryland across the Potowmack to the Evan Watkins landing, about 250 yards southeast. This landing was also the entrance of Braddock's Road into what is now Berkeley County, West Virginia, where Washington and Braddock crossed in 1755 on their way to Fort Duquesne. To the northeast is Maidstone-on-the-Potomac, home of Evan Watkins, 1744.

US 11, near Berkeley-Maryland border

HEDGESVILLE

Site of stockade fort built during the early Indian wars. Mt. Zion Episcopal Church was built soon after. A mile west is the tavern, built, 1740-1750, by Robert Snodgrass on land patented in 1732 by William Snodgrass, pioneer settler.

WV 9, Hedgesville

"MORGAN'S ACRES"

Two miles west is the site of the first house in present West Virginia. It was built by Col. Morgan Morgan who came from Delaware in 1726. It was destroyed and the one now there was built in 1800 by another Morgan.

US 11, in Morgan Park, Bunker Hill

MORGAN MORGAN

Morgan Morgan, a native of Wales, established his home at Bunker Hill before 1732, and was leader in the Eastern Panhandle's early development. His sons gave name to Morgantown, and fought in Indian and Revolutionary wars.

US 11, in Morgan Park, Bunker Hill

MORGAN CABIN

Originally built 1731-34 as second home of Morgan Morgan—first white settler in West Virginia. Rebuilt with some of original logs in 1976 as a State and County Bicentennial project. It was here during the Revolution that James Morgan, the grandson of Col. Morgan Morgan, was shot and killed by a group of Tories. Since then, this area has been known as Torytown.

County Route 26, 2.2 miles west of US 11, Bunker Hill

MORGAN'S CHAPEL

The first Episcopal Church in West Virginia. It was fostered, 1740, by Colonel Morgan Morgan, an early immigrant from Wales, who estab-

13

lished his home here. The present structure, built in 1851, is still used as a place of worship.

US 11 and County Route 26, Bunker Hill

DARKESVILLE

Named for Gen. William Darke, veteran of the Revolution and the Indian wars. He saved the remnants of St. Clair's army from massacre in 1791 when badly defeated by the Miami Indians. His son, Capt. Joseph Darke, lost his life.

US 11, Darkesville

GERRARDSTOWN

Established as a town, 1787. Named for John Gerrard, first pastor of Mill Creek Baptist Church, which was organized by early settlers about 1743. The congregation reorganized after Indian hostilities during the French and Indian War.

WV 51, west of junction with County Route 51/5, Gerrardstown

GERARD HOUSE

Built by John Hays, 1743. Became home of Reverend David Gerard, who founded Gerrardstown in 1787. His father was Reverend John Gerard, the first Baptist Minister west of the Blue Ridge Mountains.

County Route 51/2, 0.1 miles south of junction with WV 51, Gerrardstown

BOONE COUNTY

Formed, 1847, from Cabell, Kanawha, and Logan. Named for

Daniel Boone, noted hunter and explorer, who made his home in the Great Kanawha Valley, 1788-1795. In 1791, he was a member of the Virginia Assembly from Kanawha.

*US 119, Boone-Kanawha border; WV 94, Boone-Kanawha border; *WV 3, Boone-Lincoln border; *US 119, Boone-Logan border; *WV 3, Boone-Raleigh border; *WV 85, Boone-Wyoming border*

MADISON

County seat, incorporated in 1906 and named for William Madison Peyton, a leader in movement for the formation of Boone County, 1847. Peyton, pioneer in the development of the Coal River Valley, locked and dammed Coal River in the 1840's and made it navigable for steamboats to transport coal from area to markets, and for a period made the Coal Valley one of the great industrial regions of the State.

WV 85, courthouse square, Madison

INDIAN CAMP

Under rock overhang across highway was an Indian camp site. Here were found several burials. One occupation, Fort Ancient, dates from A.D. 1400; another, Buck Garden, from A.D. 1000. Pottery and other artifacts were found.

WV 3, Drawdy Falls Park, just west of Peytona

PEYTONA

Named for William Madison Peyton, father of navigation on Coal River, who promoted and actively

Boone County is named for frontiersman Daniel Boone, who lived in the Kanawha Valley from 1788 to 1795.

engaged in coal mining. As chief engineer for the Coal River Navigation Company, he locked and dammed Coal River in the 1840's and made it navigable for steamboats to transport cannel coal from the Peytona mines to distant markets of the world. The maximum annual output from these mines was approximately 200,000 tons.

WV 3, Drawdy Falls Park, just west of Peytona

JOHN EDWARD KENNA
To the north, birthplace and home of John Edward Kenna, U.S. Senator and prominent figure in the early life of this State. His statue stands among the notables of other States in the Hall of Columns in the national capitol in Washington.

WV 3, Drawdy Falls Park, just west of Peytona

COAL DISCOVERED
John Peter Salley (Salling) and companions discovered coal near here in 1742 on their exploring trip from the Greenbrier River. They followed the Coal River to its junction with

The Great Kanawha River at St. Albans.

WV 3, Racine Community Center/John Slack Park, Racine

BRAXTON COUNTY
Formed, 1836, from Kanawha, Lewis, and Nicholas. Named for Carter Braxton, one of the signers of the Declaration of Independence. Washington planned to establish important point in project for western communication in this county.

*WV 4, Braxton-Clay border; WV 5, Braxton-Gilmer border; US 19/WV 4, Braxton-Lewis border; *US 19, Braxton-Nicholas border*

BIG DUNKARD-BURNING SPRINGS SAND
The Mahoning Sandstone forming the cliffs and the Freeport Sandstone forming the Falls of the Little Kanawha River respectively are the "Big Dunkard and Burning Springs Sands" of the driller. These sandstones yield oil and natural gas in West Virginia.

**US 119, north of Falls Mill*

The Boone County Courthouse in Madison, completed in 1921

"Crossing Little Birch River to Bulltown," by J. Nep Roesler

BULLTOWN/BULLTOWN BATTLE

Important point in plan of Washington to establish water transportation to West. Salt was made here as early as 1792. Attack of whites in 1772 upon Captain Bull's Indian village here was among the causes of Dunmore's War.

On October 13, 1863, a force of 400 Union troops under Captain W.H. Mattingly, entrenched on the hills to the northeast, repulsed attack of Confederate forces under Colonel W.L. Jackson. Jackson retreated, after some loss, into Pocahontas County.

US 19, about 2 miles west of Falls Mill

SUTTON

Named for its founder. Burned, 1861, by Confederate troops. First settlers in this county were Jeremiah and Benjamin Carpenter, who had settled on Elk River, 1784. Soon after, Benjamin and wife were killed by the Indians.

County Route 19/40 (Main Street), Sutton

GEOGRAPHIC CENTER

The geographic center of the irregular-shaped state of West Virginia is near this point, according to accepted methods of locating centers of geographic areas. It was also West Virginia's center of population in 1860.

Elk River Hunting Area Road, Bakers Run, south of Sutton

Downtown Sutton, 1930s

17

BROOKE COUNTY

Formed in 1797 from Ohio County. Named for Robert Brooke, Virginia governor, 1794-1796. Here Alexander Campbell founded the Christian Church and established a college. First Grimes Golden apple tree in this county.

*WV 2, Brooke-Hancock border; *WV 88, Brooke-Ohio border; *WV 2, Brooke-Ohio border; US 22, Brooke-Ohio state border; WV 27, Brooke-Pennsylvania border*

ST. JOHN'S EPISCOPAL CHURCH

Founded in 1793 by Joseph Doddridge. It is the first Episcopal Church west of the Alleghenies and the oldest continuous worshipping congregation within this religious body in West Virginia. The first church, made of logs, was burned by Indians. Little is known about the second church. The present colonial structure was built in 1849 with hand-hewn stone foundation, handmade bricks, original cherry floor and box pews.

WV Alternate 27, near Follansbee

FORT DECKER

John Decker built (1774) a fort of logs and stone on a site just north of State St., near the Ohio River. Leaden bullets and arrowheads found here on the river bank signify fort was attacked by Indians from Mingo Island.

*Main Street north of State Street on public playground, Follansbee

GEORGE WASHINGTON CROSSING 1770

George Washington began a journey on October 5, 1770 to the Ohio Country to see lands he had fought to win and now hoped to own. After a trip, on November 3, up the Kanawha River, the party headed back up the Ohio River. On November 17, they reached Mingo Town. Three days later their horses arrived. The party then crossed the river here and traveled on across West Virginia's northern panhandle to Fort Pitt.

*WV 2, near Cross Creek Bridge

MURPHY AND COW RUN SANDS

The Morgantown (top) and the Saltsburg (bottom) sandstones, the "Murphy and Cow Run Sands", respectively of the driller, are exposed in the cliff to the east. The "Murphy" produces oil in Lewis County and the "Cow Run" produces oil and natural gas in northern West Virginia.

*WV 2, near Cross Creek

BEECH BOTTOM FORT

Near here stood Beech Bottom Fort, which was with Fort Pitt and Fort Henry in the group of posts guarding the western borders during the Revolution and its attendant Indian wars. Troops from Fort Pitt helped garrison this important fort.

WV 2, Beech Bottom

18

View of Wellsburg, circa 1900

WELLSBURG
Established in 1791. Brooke Academy, started, 1778, incorporated in 1799. Here lived Joseph Doddridge, the author of "Frontier Notes," and Patrick Gass, member of the Lewis and Clark Expedition and author of its Journal.

WV 2, Wellsburg

ISAAC DUVALL AND COMPANY
The first glass house in Western Virginia was built at Charlestown, now Wellsburg, in 1813, by Isaac Taylor Duvall and Company. It was located on the southeast corner of Fifth and Yankee Streets. Cobalt blue, green and clear flint glass wares were made here. Isaac Duvall died in 1828, and company was sold in 1838 to Samuel Lowther, Joseph Miller and George Cotts for $2100.

WV 2, Wellsburg

MILLER'S TAVERN
Built by John Henderson prior to 1798 in Federal style, the building was leased by William Miller and operated as a tavern for 50 years. Since 1974 building has housed the Brooke County Museum.

Northeast corner of Main and 6th streets, Wellsburg

WELLSBURG WHARF
In the 1790's flatboats left here with their cargos for southern markets. To accommodate and store products, warehouses and wharfs were built along our river banks. This wharf, which was established in the 1800's, extended twenty feet out in the river. To the north and south of this wharf are the foundations of two warehouses which were built in the 1790's and the early 1800's.

West end of 6th Street, at junction with Main Street, Wellsburg

OLD JAIL AND MUSEUM
Old County Jail built in 1893 houses the Brooke County Historical Museum, founded 1969. The Lloyd Furniture Factory, destroyed by fire, 1873, occupied the site. Some articles of furniture made in this factory are in museum.

*Wellsburg

GRIMES GOLDEN APPLE
Watering trough marks location of first Grimes Golden Apple tree, discovered by owner of land, Thomas Grimes, in 1802. Memorial Trough sponsored by the Franklin Country Women's Club in 1922.

WV 27 (Washington Pike), roadside park, 2.5 miles east of Wellsburg

DROVERS INN

Constructed by John Fowler, 1848-51 with bricks fired on the property. First known as Fowler's Inn, the house provided food and lodging for drovers herding livestock over the Wellsburg-Washington Turnpike to eastern markets. Other services provided at the Inn included a post office, general store and livestock yards. Fowler also operated a steam powered grist mill in the area.

WV 27, (Washington Pike), 3.5 miles east of Wellsburg

TOLLGATE HOUSE

One of two tollgate houses erected by the Wellsburg and Washington Turnpike Company in 1834. Served taking tolls on the Pike until 1910. The other tollgate house was located one-half mile east of Wellsburg and was torn down when the Pike was rebuilt in the 1930's. House located here is now owned by Brooke Hills Park and is occupied as a residence.

WV 27 (Washington Pike), 4.5 miles east of Wellsburg at entrance to Brooke Hills Park

BETHANY TURNPIKE TUNNELS

First highway tunnels constructed west of Alleghenies. They were built in 1831 by Richard Waugh at personal expense to ease transportation to his flour mills. The tunnels, a mile apart, were removed by the State in 1957.

WV 67, 3 miles east of Wellsburg

WAUGH FLOUR MILLS

Four flour mills were constructed near Wellsburg in the early 1800s. The first of these mills was built by John Moore in 1800. Moore's son-in-law, Richard Waugh, built the old stone mill in 1824, and the upper mill in 1835. A.M. Buchanan built the fourth mill in 1847. This mill was owned and operated by James, David and Ashley Waugh until 1924. It was destroyed by fire in 1931.

WV 67, 3 miles east of Wellsburg

RICE'S FORT/BETHANY

Near here stood the frontier outpost built by Abraham and Daniel Rice on Buffalo Creek. In September, 1782, its little garrison of six men repulsed an attack of 100 Indians, who had just been defeated in an assault on Fort Henry, Wheeling.

Bethany College established here in 1840, oldest school of college rank in State. The home and the study of Alexander Campbell, founder, are here. Prof. A.E. Dolbear here perfected parts of the telephone, which Bell used.

WV 67, Bethany

BETHANY COLLEGE/BETHANY

Oldest degree granting institution in West Virginia, the College was chartered in the Old Dominion in 1840, succeeding Buffalo Seminary established by Alexander Campbell in 1818. Remaining open through the Civil War, it was the only college operating in the new state in 1863. Women were admitted in 1877 and the school was

Alexander Campbell

among the earliest accredited colleges in the nation.

Here Scots-Irish Alexander Campbell founded a religious movement which he called the Disciples of Christ. In this place Amos Dolbear perfected parts of the telephone, and longtime Speaker of the House "Champ" Clark, Supreme Court Justice Joseph Lamar and benefactor Earl Oglebay studied. Here James A. Garfield was a Trustee and John F. Kennedy affirmed belief in separation of church and state.

WV 67 (Main Street), at intersection with College Street, Bethany

BETHANY CHURCH OF CHRIST

Bethany Church of Christ, the oldest church building in Bethany, was built in 1852 according to plans drawn by Alexander Campbell, founder of Bethany College and leader in the Disciples Movement. Its foundation is built of stone from the original church erected on this site in 1832. Bethany Church was organized as a separate congregation

in 1829. Campbell was pastor for many years, while serving as president of Bethany College.

WV 67 (Main Street), near church building and cemetery, Bethany

DELTA TAU DELTA BIRTHPLACE

In this house, 8 Bethany College Students—William Cunningham, John Johnson, Alexander Earle, Richard Alfred, Eugene Tarr, Henry Bell, John Hunt and Jacob Lowe—Met in 1858 and founded Delta Tau Delta. This social fraternity soon spread across the American Continent. In 1977, plans were completed for the restoration of this structure to its original condition.

WV 67, Bethany

CAMPBELL CEMETERY

Here are buried the Campbell family; the first missionaries, other prominent leaders in the Disciples Movement, presidents and distinguished teachers of Bethany College. The seven foot hand hewed stone wall is a unique feature of Cemetery.

WV 67, 0.5 miles east of Bethany at cemetery entrance

ALEXANDER CAMPBELL

Here lived the leading influence in America's largest indigenous religious movement, Christian Church (Disciples of Christ), and founder of Bethany College. Built in four periods: the John Brown Mansion, completed 1793; Buffalo Seminary, in 1819; brick dining wing in 1836; and "Stranger's Hall", in 1840.

Among famous Americans who were guests were Calhoun, Clay, Webster, Davis, Garfield.

WV 67, 0.5 miles east of Bethany

CABELL COUNTY

Formed, 1809, from Kanawha. Originally included several of the present counties of West Virginia. Named for William H. Cabell, Virginia governor, 1805-08. Big Sandy River was the western end of the James River and Kanawha Turnpike.

*WV 10, Cabell-Lincoln border; *WV 2, Cabell-Mason border; *US 60, Cabell-Putnam border; US 60, Cabell-Wayne border; *WV 152, Cabell-Wayne border

GENERAL JENKINS

"Greenbottom" (N.E.) was home of General Albert G. Jenkins, brilliant Confederate officer, mortally wounded at Cloyd's Mountain in 1864. On raid in Sept. 1862, Jenkins' 8th Virginia Cavalry was first to carry Confederate flag into state of Ohio.

WV 2, 2 miles south of Mason County line, Greenbottom

SAVAGE GRANT

Boundary line of land grant surveyed under Washington's orders for John Savage and companions for service in French and Indian War. Their land lay along the Ohio and Big Sandy rivers from Louisa, Kentucky, to near Mason County line.

*WV 2, near Lesage

GUYANDOTTE

Indian name. Founded in 1810. Site chosen as county seat, 1809, and court first met here, October, 1810. Important point in river traffic, connecting with the James River and Kanawha Turnpike. Burned during War between the States.

WV 2 (Bridge Street), at junction with Richmond Street, Huntington

Nineteenth century view of Guyandotte from across the Ohio River. From an 1821 painting by Felix Saint-Aulaire.

WAR BETWEEN THE STATES GENERALS/ SPRING HILL CEMETERY

Two of seven War Between the States generals buried in W.Va. interred here: Albert Gallatin Jenkins, C.S.A. in Confederate plot; John Hunt Oley, Union, and over 200 soldiers. Confederate Monument dedicated in 1900.

Many area founding families buried in 110 acre cemetery. Incls. plots for Confederate, Union, and Pallotine Sisters, Veterans' Sections, & monument honoring the Marshall Univ. football team and fans killed in 1970 plane crash.

Norway Avenue, Huntington

HUNTINGTON STATE HOSPITAL

Established in 1897 as a Home for Incurables. The name was changed in 1901 to the West Virginia Asylum and in 1916 to Huntington State Hospital. Its 698-acre farm is located on the Guyandotte River near the town of Barboursville.

*Norway Avenue and 20th Street, Huntington

MARSHALL MEMORIAL BOULEVARD

On November 14, 1970, a chartered jet crashed on approach to Tri-State Airport near Huntington, claiming the lives of seventy-five members of the Marshall University football team, coaches, fans, pilots & crew. This boulevard, named in honor of these fallen members of the univer-sity family, leads visitors from the Spring Hill Cemetery to the heart of the Marshall community.

20th Street, at junction with Norway Avenue, Huntington; 20th Street and 3rd Avenue, Huntington

MARSHALL UNIVERSITY

Named for John Marshall, Chief Justice U.S. Supreme Court, 1801-1835. Founded as Marshall Academy, 1837, and chartered as Marshall College, 1858. Established as a state-supported institution, 1867. Granted university status, 1961.

3rd Avenue and 18th Street, Huntington; US 60 (5th Avenue), near junction with Hal Greer Boulevard, Huntington; Hal Greer Boulevard, at junction with 4th Avenue, Huntington

B&O RAILROAD DEPOT/ HERITAGE VILLAGE

Passenger station completed 1887, freighthouses 1890 with additions 1898, 1911 & 1916. B&O, oldest U.S. line, acquired in 1901. Superior location in business district gave B&O edge over C&O in city.

Opened in 1977, historic structures are adapted to modern retail uses based on theme of railroad heritage. Includes B&O Depot, an 1875 Bank and Gutzon Borglum statue of city founder Collis Huntington.

11th Street, between Veterans Memorial Boulevard and 3rd Avenue, Huntington

Huntington's Fourth Avenue commercial district, early 1960s

HUNTINGTON

Originally called Holderby's Landing. Laid out as a town, 1869, by Collis P. Huntington of the C&O Railroad, and named for him when incorporated, 1871. Western end of C&O when the first trains came from Richmond in 1873.

US 60 (5th Avenue), between 7th and 8th streets, Huntington

JAMES RIVER COMPANY

George Washington was made president in 1785 of the James River Company. His plan of communication to the West eventually resulted in the construction of the Midland Trail, U.S. 60, and the Chesapeake and Ohio Railroad.

US 60 (5th Avenue), at junction with 6th Street, Huntington

BARBOURSVILLE STATE HOSPITAL

Established as Barboursville Unit of Weston State Hospital, 1942, on property once used by Morris Harvey College. In 1947, became Unit of Huntington State Hospital. In 1949, by legislative act, it became Barboursville State Hospital.

*US 60, Barboursville

BARBOURSVILLE

Established, 1813. County seat moved here from Guyandotte and remained until taken to Huntington in 1887. Before the Guyandotte courthouse was chosen, court met

24

at the home of William Merritt, 1809-1810, on Mud River near here.

Main Street, at junction with Water Street, Barboursville

WOODY WILLIAMS BRIDGE
Bridge named for Hershel "Woody" Williams, who as a corporal in 3rd Marine Div. during World War II won Congressional Medal of Honor for his heroism against the Japanese at Iwo Jima, 23 Feb. 1945.

US 60, at junction with County Route 19 (Merritts Creek Road), Barboursville

OLD TOLL HOUSE
This Old Toll House, built in 1837, stood below town of Barboursville on Guyan River bank; tolls collected on James River-Kanawha Turnpike from those using ferry. Restored in 1950 by the D.A.R., Barboursville.

Main Street, near junction with Mohawk Street, Barboursville

THE BRYAN FAMILY
North of here (1826-28) lived John and Nancy Bryan, grandparents of William J. Bryan, the Great Commoner. They moved to Gallipolis Ferry where they died; John, 1834; Nancy in 1832. Buried nearby in the Yatesmont Cemetery.

US 60, Kiwanivista Park, 0.7 miles west of Ona

UNION BAPTIST CHURCH
Church completed, 1849. Occupied during the War Between the States by a Federal garrison to protect the

one-lane covered bridge, which was a vital link in the James River and Kanawha Turnpike. The soldiers left the Church in shambles. It has been restored but bayonet marks, bullet pock-marks, gallery for slaves can still be seen. Nearby the earthworks are visible.

County Route 25/7 (Fair Grounds Road), Milton

HARSHBARGER CORNER
Survey of Milton began here in 1872 and post office was established in 1873. Founder, David Harshbarger, later lived on this lot. Named for Milton Reece, first postmaster and large landholder in vicinity. Town incorporated 1876 with Captain J.R. Burke as first mayor. Captain John Harshbarger occupied a log house 60 feet to north and operated a grist mill to the southwest on Mud River.

US 60, at junction with County Route 25/7 (Fair Grounds Road), Milton

MUD RIVER COVERED BRIDGE
Erected in 1875 by order of the Cabell Co. Court. The contract was awarded to R.H. Baker, the local postmaster. This design was developed by bridge engineer William Howe in 1840. Length is 112 feet.

East Mud River Road, 0.2 miles south of US 60, Milton

SALT ROCK
First white settlers came here from Giles County, Virginia in pursuit of an Indian raiding party that had taken their horses. Permanent settle-

ment established by 1800. McComas and Hatfield families were among first settlers. Thomas Ward produced salt here as early as 1817, and it soon became a major industry in area. Legend says that community was named because farmers here used to put salt on the rocks along the river to induce their cattle to come and drink. Petroglyphs, village sites, mounds and artifacts found nearby indicate the presence of Indians as early as 1000 A.D.

County Route 45 (Roach Road), Salt Rock Community Park, Salt Rock

CALHOUN COUNTY

Named for John C. Calhoun, eminent statesman from South Carolina. Is an important oil and gas producing county. It is largely devoted to farming and has been prominent in livestock raising.

*WV 16, Calhoun-Clay border; *WV 5, Calhoun-Gilmer border; *US 33, Calhoun-Gilmer border; WV 16, Calhoun-Ritchie border; *US 33, Calhoun-Roane border; *WV 5, Calhoun-Wirt border*

FIRST COUNTY COURT
Site of first Calhoun Co. Court which met at home of Joseph Burson, April 14, 1856. Justices were Wm. Brannon, Dan. Duskey, H.R. Ferrell, Geo. Lynch, Joshua Knight, Absalom Knotts and Hiram Ferrell.

WV 5, 0.1 miles from junction with County Route 1, 2 miles west of Bigbend

GRANTSVILLE
Town was laid out in 1866 on farm of Simon P. Stump and named for Gen. Grant. Became permanent

1912 flood damage in Grantsville, the Calhoun County seat

26

Swandale Mill in Clay County, date unknown

county seat of Calhoun in 1869, after 13 years of moving county seat from place to place. Incorporated 1896.

WV 5 (Main Street), at junction with Court Street, courthouse square, Grantsville

ARNOLDSBURG SKIRMISH

Site of Camp McDonald, set up, 1862, occupied by the 11th W.Va. Inf., U.S.V. Scene of engagement, May 6, 1862, when Federals under Major George C. Trimble beat off an attack by Confederate Moccasin Rangers under Capt. George Downs.

US 33, Arnoldsburg

GRAVE OF MIKE FINK

One mile west in the low gap are the graves of Mike Fink and an Indian, slain in 1780, and buried where they fell. While hunting, Fink and Adam O'Brien were fired on by two Indians; Fink shot one and was killed by the other.

WV 16, at junction with County Route 13, just north of Minnora

CLAY COUNTY

Formed in 1858 from Braxton and Nicholas. Named for Henry Clay, the great Kentuckian, who was so popular in western Virginia that in

1820 a monument was erected to him for his part in bringing the National Road to Wheeling.

*WV 4, Clay-Braxton border; WV 16, Clay-Calhoun border; *WV 4, Clay-Kanawha border; WV 16, Clay-Nicholas border; *WV 36, Clay-Roane border*

CLAY

Both county and county seat are named for Henry Clay. The Golden Delicious apple, once called "Mullins' Yellow Seedling," was developed on Porters Creek. This State also produced the Grimes Golden, the other great yellow apple.

WV 16, Courthouse Square, Clay

WILLIAM C. MARKLE

To E. was Claud Markle (1882-1962) home, noted road builder in Clay, Webster, Boone, & Kanawha in early 20th C. Projects incl. Maysel intersection of US 119/36 & 4, Clay Jct., Rt. 16, & Widen Ridge; bridges; tunnels; & culverts. He worked on Alaskan RR, Hoover Dam, and road in Death Valley, NV. Markle served seven years on Clay Co. Court, including term as president. He was a 32nd Degree Mason and Shriner.

Near junction of WV 4 and WV 16, west of Clay

DODDRIDGE COUNTY

Formed in 1845 from Ritchie, Harrison, Tyler and Lewis. Named for Philip Doddridge, lawyer-statesman of western Virginia. Many of the Indians who once came to this State got war and hunting weapons from flint quarries near by.

*WV 18, Doddridge-Gilmer border; *US 50, Doddridge-Harrison border; WV 23, Doddridge-Harrison border; County Route 50/30 (Old US 50), Doddridge-Ritchie border; *WV 18, Doddridge-Tyler border; *WV 23, Doddridge-Tyler border*

GREENBRIER CHURCH & CEMETERY

Site of Greenbrier Seventh Day Baptist Church, organized Aug. 1870 by members of New Salem church, est. 1792 in Salem. Met in log building; new church dedicated, 1880; razed, 1975. Rev. Peter Davis (1783-1885), original settler & Rev. Jacob Davis (1827-85), first pastor, buried here. Pulpit, pews & window panes used in Fort New Salem meeting house at Salem-Teikyo University.

County Route 17 (Greenbrier Road), 3.5 miles south of Salem

CENTER POINT COVERED BRIDGE

This privately owned covered bridge was completed in 1890 as ordered by the county court. Stone masons T.C. Ancell and E. Underwood prepared all abutments at a cost of $976.54, and carpenters John Ash and S.H. Smith built frame superstructure for $230. Span, 12 1/2' wide and 42' long, constructed according to truss design developed by Stephen Long, crosses the Middle Fork of McElroy Creek.

WV 23, Center Point

Matthew M. Neely
21st governor of West Virginia

WEST UNION

West Union, incorporated in 1881, was formerly called Lewisport in honor of Lewis Maxwell. It is the county seat of Doddridge, named for Philip Doddridge. In it lived J.H. Diss Debar and Sen. and Gov. Matthew M. Neely.

WV 18, 0.6 miles north of junction with US 50, West Union

MATTHEW M. NEELY

21st governor of W.Va. (1941-1945), born at Grove, 1874, spent boyhood here in former town of Market. He served in Spanish American War and graduated from W.Va. Univ. before opening law practice in Fairmont. His public career included terms as mayor of Fairmont & clerk of House of Delegates. Elected to 5 terms in U.S. House & Senate (1912-58), he died while in the Senate at age 83.

WV 18, at junction with County Route 13 (Maxwell Ridge Road), Market

J.H. DISS DEBAR

Here lived Joseph H. Diss Debar, artist, designer of the State seal and coat of arms. He lived here many years and helped establish Saint Clara Colony nearby, about 1845. Author of first "Handbook of West Virginia".

WV 18, near junction with County Route 66 (Camp Run Road), near Leopold

FAYETTE COUNTY

Formed in 1831 from Nicholas, Greenbrier, Kanawha, Logan. Named for General Lafayette. On New River, 1671, Batts and Fallam officially claimed Mississippi Valley for Great Britain in opposition to the claim of France.

*WV 20, Fayette-Greenbrier border; *US 60, Fayette-Greenbrier border; WV 61, Fayette-Kanawha border; US 60, Fayette-Kanawha border; *US 19, Fayette-Nicholas border; *WV 39, Fayette-Nicholas border; *WV 61, Fayette-Raleigh border; WV 41, Fayette-Raleigh border; *US 19/ WV 16, Fayette-Raleigh border; WV 20, Fayette-Summers border*

MONTGOMERY

Settled before the Revolution by Levi Morris, whose father, William Morris, made the first permanent settlement in the Great Kanawha Valley. Named Coal Valley in 1879. Renamed for James C. Montgomery when incorporated in 1891.

WV 61, at the bridge, Montgomery

WEST VIRGINIA INSTITUTE OF TECHNOLOGY

State institution established in 1895 as Preparatory Branch of West Virginia University. In 1931, name was changed to New River State College. Became a multipurpose college in 1941, known as West Virginia Institute of Technology.

WV 61, Montgomery

ANCIENT WORKS

On a ridge between Armstrong and Loop creeks across the river are extensive prehistoric stone ruins whose walls are several miles long, and enclose a large area. Many of these stones are from the valley below the old wall.

US 60, Boomer

INDIAN VILLAGE/INDIAN WALLS

In the bottomland towards Kanawha River was an extensive Indian village site. Excavations, 1961-62, established three main occupations: a Hopewellian one of about A.D. 500, a later Woodland Indian one of about A.D. 1000, and finally a Fort Ancient (probably Shawnee) town of about A.D. 1500. Over 60 burials have been recorded from the village area as well as many storage pits, and evidence of houses and palisades.

On the summit of Armstrong Mountain to the south are found the "mystery walls", short windrows of rock straddling the mountain's flat top. They were probably constructed between A.D. 1 and 500 by Hopewellian peoples of the village in the bottom. Their function is unknown, but was probably ceremonial. Kanawha black flint stratum occurs below the walls and was quarried by Indians. Flint workshop areas are found on the mountaintop.

WV 61, 4 miles south of Montgomery

CAMP REYNOLDS

Located across Kanawha River from this point was Civil War camp for Union Army, 1862-64. Site had 56 cabins and parade grounds for 23rd Ohio Vol. Inf. commanded by Col. Rutherford B. Hayes and Lt. William McKinley, future United States presidents.

US 60, Glen Ferris Inn parking area, Glen Ferris

GAULEY BRIDGE

Here New and Gauley rivers unite to form Great Kanawha River. Piers still stand of old bridge destroyed by the Confederate troops in 1861. Here Thomas Dunn English, author of the ballad, "Ben Bolt", wrote "Gauley River".

US 60, Gauley Bridge

HAWK'S NEST

Once called Marshall's Pillar for Chief Justice John Marshall, who came here, 1812. U.S. engineers declare the New River Canyon, 585 feet deep, surpasses the famed Royal Gorge. Tunnel for river makes vast water power here.

US 60, Hawks Nest State Park

Suspension bridge across the Gauley River, 1862. This bridge was constructed by Union troops to replace one destroyed during a skirmish in September 1861.

HAWK'S NEST TUNNEL

Mouth of the great Hawk's Nest Tunnel, three miles long, which diverts water of New River from its five-mile long gorge. The tunnel, a mile of which is through solid rock, and a 50-foot dam give waterfall of 160 feet for electric power.

*US 60, 0.8 miles east of Gauley Bridge

HAWK'S NEST TUNNEL DISASTER

Construction of nearby tunnel, diverting waters of New R. through Gauley Mt. for hydroelectric power, resulted in state's worst industrial disaster. Silica rock dust caused 109 admitted deaths in mostly black, migrant underground work force of 3,000. Congressional hearing placed toll at 476 for 1930-35. Tragedy brought recognition of acute silicosis as occupational lung disease and compensation legislation to protect workers.

US 60, Hawks Nest State Park

SALT SAND

The sheer cliffs of Nuttall sandstones forming the walls of the New River Gorge are the "Salt Sands" of the driller. These sands produce oil and natural gas in West Virginia and commercial brines on the Kanawha and Ohio Rivers.

US 60, Hawks Nest State Park, Fayette County

"CONTENTMENT"

Built, 1830, on the old James River and Kanawha Turnpike. Restored antebellum home of Colonel George W. Imboden, on General Lee's staff,

31

Construction of the Hawks Nest Tunnel in the early 1930s resulted in one of the nation's worst industrial disasters.

C.S.A. Property and headquarters of the Fayette County Historical Society, organized in 1926.

US 60, in front of Contentment Museum, Ansted

JACKSON'S MOTHER
In Westlake Cemetery is the grave of the mother of General Thomas J. "Stonewall" Jackson. The monument at the grave was placed by Captain Thomas Ranson, who had fought in Jackson's old brigade in the War between the States.

Westlake Cemetery, Cemetery Street, Ansted

"HALFWAY HOUSE"
Regular stop on the James River and Kanawha Turnpike. The original building, dating from before the Revolution, was rebuilt by William Tyree, 1810. During the winter of 1861-62, it was headquarters for Chicago Gray Dragoons.

*US 60, east end of Ansted

FAYETTEVILLE
In the attack on Federal forces here, 1863, Milton W. Humphreys, the educator and soldier, gunner of Bryan's Battery, 13th Virginia Light Artillery, C.S.A., first used "indirect firing," now in universal military use.

Court Street, in front of courthouse, Fayetteville

FAYETTEVILLE TOWN PARK
Memorial Park was presented to citizens of Fayetteville to honor all veterans who served to defend their country. LaFayette Post No. 149, The American Legion, obtained lease for this property on August 4, 1958 from the New River Pocahontas Coal Co. On November 6, 1972, Berwind Land Co., a holding company, with Lafayette Post No. 149, deeded the 11.42 acres to the town of Fayetteville for a park.

Junction of Park Drive and Sarah Street, Charlie McCoy Park, Fayetteville

INDIRECT FIRING
Nearby on May 19-20, 1863, Corp. Milton W. Humphreys, gunner in Bryan's Battery 13th Virginia Light Artillery, C.S.A., made first use of indirect artillery fire in warfare. Target was Union fort in Fayetteville.

Nickleville Road, Fayetteville

OLD STONE HOUSE
Southwest is the Old Stone House, built, 1824, by Richard Tyree on the James River and Kanawha Turnpike. It was visited by Jackson, Clay, Webster, Benton, and other notables. Here Matthew Fontaine Maury wrote his book on navigation.

US 60 at junction with County Route 10 (Stonehouse Road), 1 mile east of Hilton Village

ANDREW & CHARLES LEWIS MARCH
The nearby highway is part of route traversing W.Va. from Lewisburg to Point Pleasant memorialized by the state to commemorate the march of

4-H campers raise the flag in front of Camp Washington-Carver's Great Chestnut Lodge, date unknown.

the American Colonial army of 1,200 men led by Andrew & Charles Lewis. After a month's march this army defeated a Shawnee Indian force led by Cornstalk at the Battle of Point Pleasant on the banks of the Ohio & Kanawha rivers, October 10, 1774.

US 60, at junction with WV 41 South

CAMP WASHINGTON-CARVER
Camp named for Booker T. Washington (1856-1915) and George Washington Carver (1864-1943). Land deeded for sum of $5.00 by Charles and Kathryn Midelburg. Constructed 1939-1942 by local WPA labor with materials found on site including stone and native chestnut. Operated by W.Va. State College as Negro 4-H Camp, 1942-57.

In 1979, Legislature transferred to Department of Culture and History.

County Route 11/3, off County Route 11/4 (Clifftop Loop), near Clifftop

SPY ROCK
Sandstone formation at 2510 feet is landmark known for view of Sewell Mt. range to SE. Known as "Rock of Eyes" by Native Americans and dubbed "Spy Rock" by Civil War soldiers. Sept. 1861, Gen. J.D. Cox and 5,000 Union soldiers camped here to oppose Gen. Robert E. Lee at Sewell Mt. Site of Col. Geo. Alderson farm and tollgate on James River and Kanawha Turnpike, 1834-73. Source for name of Lookout.

US 60, just west of Lookout

GEN. ROBERT E. LEE

Near here, at highest point on the Midland Trail, Gen. Robert E. Lee had headquarters during his campaign in West Virginia in 1861. His famous war horse, "Traveler," was brought to him here from the Andrew Johnston farm in Greenbrier County.

US 60, 2.25 miles west of Greenbrier County border

GILMER COUNTY

Formed, 1845, from Kanawha and Lewis. Named for Thomas Walker Gilmer, Secretary of the Navy in President Tyler's Cabinet, who was killed by the explosion of a gun on board the United States battleship, Princeton, February 28, 1844.

*WV 5, Gilmer-Braxton border; *WV 5, Gilmer-Calhoun border; *US 33, Gilmer-Calhoun border; WV 18, Gilmer-Doddridge border; US 33, Gilmer-Lewis border; *WV 47, Gilmer-Ritchie border*

JOB'S TEMPLE

Begun in 1860 and completed after the Civil War, this handhewn log church building is oldest in Gilmer County. Job's Temple Class of the Methodist Episcopal Church South was organized by the Rev. G.S. McCutchen, first pastor in 1866. First trustees were: Levi Snider, William, Salathiel and N.W. Stalnaker, James Pickens, Edward Gainer and Christian Kuhl. Placed on National Register in 1979.

WV 5, near junction with County Route 35/4 (Job's Run Road)

SITE OF FIRST GILMER COURT

On 24 March 1845, Commissioners met here in Salathiel Stalnaker's brick home to organize Gilmer County from parts of Lewis and Kanawha. Members were: Bennett, Conrad, Hayes, Stump, Riddle, Arnold, Huffman, Cook, Maze, Benson, Knotts, Holt, Norman, Cox & Stalnaker. Voters, by majority of 66, moved county seat from Dekalb site to the "Ford," later named Glenville. In 1880s, damaged by flooding, home was razed.

WV 5, 0.2 miles from junction with County Route 24/2 (Millseat Run Road), 8.9 miles west of Glenville

ENGLE HOMESTEAD

Nearby is the homestead of Henry Everett Engle (1849-1933) where in 1885 he composed the melody for "The West Virginia Hills," the most popular of the official state songs of West Virginia.

WV 5, near junction with County Route 20 (Tanner Creek Road), Tanner

FORT MOORE

At top of the hill is the site of a log fort 30x30 feet in size, built in spring, 1864, for Capt. W.T. Wiant's Gilmer County Home Guards. Occupied until December, 1864. Burned days later by Confederates under Capt. Sida Campbell.

College Campus, Glenville

Spanish-American War recruits parade through the streets of Glenville, circa 1898.

GLENVILLE

Here was written "The West Virginia Hills", State song. This was the home of William Perry Brown, author of three score books for children, and for many years one of the most popular writers for the old "Youth's Companion".

US 33/US 119 and WV 5, Glenville

GLENVILLE STATE COLLEGE

A college that offers both professional and general education with emphasis on teacher education was established by the Legislature in 1872 as the Glenville Branch of the West Virginia Normal School. Became Glenville State Normal School 1898. Became the Glenville State Teachers College in 1930 with four-year degree granting status. The present name was approved in 1943 by the Legislature.

Robert F. Kidd Library, Glenville State College, Glenville

GLENVILLE STATE TEACHERS COLLEGE

A central West Virginia college maintained for the training of grade and high school teachers. Established as a normal school in 1872 by the Legislature. Given college status in 1930.

Administration building, Glenville State College, Glenville

WV 5, near junction with County Route 30, 3 miles east of Glenville

SAMUEL LEWIS HAYS

Built this home in 1837 on a 1000-acre tract, and laid out the town of Glenville in 1845. As a member of the Virginia Assembly, he urged the building of the Parkersburg-Staunton Turnpike. As a Congressman, in 1842, Hays appointed Thomas Jonathan (Stonewall) Jackson as a cadet to West Point. President Buchanan named Hays as Receiver of Public Moneys, 1857-60, Sauk Rapids, Minn. Died, 1871, and was buried there.

US 33/US 119, near junction with WV 5, near Glenville

DUCK RUN SUSPENSION BRIDGE

1922-1992. Funds raised and labor provided by Duck Run & Bear Run citizens Summers, Keith, Bush, Floyd Langford, Hess, Hardman, Divers, Simmons, Clovis, Wilfong, Wright. Engineers: Fred Lewis & Wm Moss. Wire cables and steel came from Roebling Co. & Bethlehem Steel. Deck lumber & concrete for towers, locals. Span 350 ft, 7 in; width 11' 6". Placed on National Register in 1997.

GRANT COUNTY

Formed in 1866 from Hardy. Named for General Grant, later President. The Fairfax Stone, which established the limits of Lord Fairfax's lands, marks northwestern boundary. The county has many mountain peaks and beautiful scenery.

US 220, Grant-Hardy border; *WV 93, Grant-Mineral border; *US 50/WV 42, Grant-Mineral border; *WV 28, Grant-Pendleton border; US 220, Grant-Pendleton border; *WV 90, Grant-Tucker border; *US 50, Grant-Maryland border

VINCENT WILLIAMS

Northeast, cabin of Vincent Williams, an early settler and noted Indian fighter of the South Branch. When his home was attacked, Williams killed five Indians before he was shot in the back by the two remaining savages.

WV 42, approximately 1 mile north of junction with County Route 5 (Patterson Creek Road), and approximately 4 miles north of junction with WV 28/WV 55

ORISKANY-HELDERBERG SANDS

The massive sandstone forming the top of the great arch is the Oriskany and the limestone below it is the Helderberg of the driller and geologist. These "sands" produce natural gas in West Virginia.

*US 220, 2 miles east of Petersburg

The cliffs of Petersburg Gap served as a backdrop for this 1902 event.

PETERSBURG

Settled about 1745. Near by was Fort George, Indian fort. Federal trenches overlooked the town in 1863 and 1864. Here is grave of Rev. W.N. Scott, pioneer preacher, who built churches at Old Fields, Moorefield, and Petersburg.

US 220/WV 28, at junction with Pepsi Lane, Petersburg

PETERSBURG GAP

Here the South Branch of the Potomac cuts through Orr's Mountain. The "Pictured Rocks", great cliffs on which appear figures of a fox and an ox or buffalo, are features. Cliffs on the south side rise to sheer heights of 800 feet.

*US 220/WV 28, Grant County

FAIRFAX LINE

Here was the southwestern boundary of the six million-acre estate of Lord Fairfax. This vast tract, lying south of the Potomac and known as the Northern Neck, included the Eastern Panhandle and most of the South Branch.

*US 220, 1 mile south of Petersburg

FORT BINGAMON

Near this fort, established as defense against Indians, stood Samuel Bingamon's cabin. His home attacked and his wife wounded, Bingamon single-handed shot and clubbed to death all but one of a party of seven Indians.

US 220, at Pansy Roadside Rest Area, south of Petersburg

ORISKANY SAND

The massive sandstone forming the top of the exposure and the great arch is the Oriskany, and the limestone below it is the Helderberg of the driller and geologist. The "Oriskany Sand", an important gas sand, has produced in excess of a trillion cubic feet of gas in West Virginia.

WV 28/WV 55, near Grant-Pendleton border

POPULATION CENTER

The population center of the United States was in present West Virginia four times as it moved westward across the nation: near Wardensville in 1820; at Smoke Hole in 1830; west of Buckhannon in 1840; near Burning Springs in 1850.

WV 28/WV 55, near Smoke Hole Road

SMOKE HOLE

Smoke Hole, a rugged canyon formed by the South Branch of the Potomac River, extends eighteen miles south to U.S. 220. Early explorers reported that heavy mists rising from the canyon looked like smoke coming from a deep hole. The canyon contains many caves and spectacular rock formations. Among the many caves, is Smoke Hole Cave. Its name originates from the presence of smoke stains on the roof which may have been caused by Indian campfires.

WV 28/WV 55 and Smoke Hole Road

TUSCARORA (CLINTON) SAND

The massive resistant Tuscarora Sandstone is vertical here and forms the top of the great arch (North Fork Gap). The "Tuscarora (Clinton) Sand" produces some gas, although it is largely untested in West Virginia.

WV 28/WV 55, near Smoke Hole Caverns

Greenland Gap, circa 1900

GREENLAND GAP

Cliffs 800 feet high lining great cleft in the New Creek and Knobley mountains, which rival the famed Franconia Notch of New England. Scene of skirmish in 1863 between General Jones' cavalry and Federal troops from New Creek.

WV 93, at junction with County Route 1 (Greenland Road), just north of junction with WV 42, Scherr

BY KING'S COMMAND

The proclamation of George III, King of England, in 1763 ordered settlement west of these mountains to stop. The early treaties between the English and the Six Nations accepted this range as the dividing line between them.

US 50, east of Gormania

FORT OGDEN

Frontier defense, including blockhouse, stockade, and cabins. Part of the chain of forts established by George Washington about 1755. Point of refuge for the Bowmans, Lees, Logsdons and many other pioneer families.

US 50, 1 mile west of junction with County Route 50/2 (Cherry Ridge Road), east of Gormania

GREENBRIER COUNTY

Formed, 1778, from Botetourt and Montgomery. Named for the river which drains it. This county had many pioneer forts and saw many bloody Indian battles. Here are the world-famed White Sulphur and other mineral springs.

*WV 20, Greenbrier-Fayette border; *US 60, Greenbrier-Fayette border; WV 3, Greenbrier-Monroe border; US 219, Greenbrier-Monroe border; WV 20, Greenbrier-Nicholas border; WV 39, Greenbrier-Nicholas border; WV 39, Greenbrier-Pocahontas border; US 219, Greenbrier-Pocahontas border (2 markers); *WV 3, Greenbrier-Summers border; *US 60, Greenbrier-Virginia state border*

MEADOW RIVER LUMBER COMPANY/ UNITED METHODIST CHURCH

Established as Raine-Andrew Lumber Co. concern with purchase of 32,000 ac. (1906-08) by John & Tom Raine, namesake of Rainelle,

Employees of the Meadow River Lumber Company pose for the camera, date unknown.

founded 1908. Used logging railroad from woods to mill & Sewell Valley RR (NF&G) to C&O. 1909 mill burned 1924; 1925 triple-band mill had 30 million bf. annual capacity, 500 workers, & made finished lumber, furniture, flooring & shoe heels. Shut down 28 Dec. 1970.

Built 1914 and said to be largest building in world made entirely of chestnut. Because of Raine family's desire for only one church within town, denomination was determined by majority of Meadow River Lumber Co. workers. Served school, service and civic groups as meeting house, and once housed the public library. Educational wing with interior of wormy chestnut was added in 1930.

US 60, near junction with WV 20 South, Rainelle

RUPERT

A post office was established here in 1889 and the village was incorporated in 1945. Named for Dr. Cyrus A. Rupert (1812-1891), a prominent local physician. The first settler here was William McClung (1738-1833) who came in 1766. A soldier in the revolution, he donated two acres of land for the area's first church at Otter Creek. He is buried in the church cemetery.

US 60, at roadside park 1 mile east of Rupert

GREENBRIER GHOST

Interred in nearby cemetery is Zona Heaster Shue. Her death in 1897 was presumed natural until her spirit appeared to her mother to describe how she was killed by her husband Edward. Autopsy on the exhumed body verified the apparition's account. Edward, found guilty of murder, was sentenced to the state prison. Only known case in which testimony from ghost helped convict a murderer.

US 60 East, near junction with I-64, Sam Black Church exit

SAM BLACK UNITED METHODIST CHURCH

Built in 1901, third Otter Creek church building was dedicated in memory of the Rev. Sam Black (1813-99). Born in Rupert, he preached here in the 1880s-90s. Licensed in 1840, Black was a Methodist circuit rider for almost fifty years. Sam Black Church, a spiritual landmark, became an established place name on highway maps without a post office by the same name.

US 60 East, near junction with I-64, Sam Black Church exit

MAXON SAND

The resistant Droop Sandstone in this quarry is the "Maxon Sand" of the driller, and shows southerly dipping cross-laminations. This sand yields oil and natural gas at depths of over 1000 feet in southern and central West Virginia.

*US 60, 2.5 miles west of Alta

ANDREW & CHARLES LEWIS MARCH

The nearby highway is part of route traversing W.Va. from Lewisburg to Point Pleasant memorialized by the state to commemorate the march of the American Colonial army of 1,200 men led by Andrew & Charles Lewis. After a month's march this army defeated a Shawnee Indian force led by Cornstalk at the Battle of Point Pleasant on the banks of the Ohio & Kanawha rivers, October 10, 1774.

US 60, at junction with County Route 60/ 41 (Old Brushy Ridge Road), Alta

BORDER HEROES/FORT DONNALLY

Before the Fort Donnally attack, settlements had been warned by Philip Hammond and John Pryor, scouts at Point Pleasant, who, made up as Indians by Nonhelema, the sister of Cornstalk, passed and outran the Indians.

Built by Andrew Donnally a few miles north about 1771. Attack on this fort by 200 Indians in 1778 was second most important frontier engagement in the State. The fort was relieved by force under Col. John Stuart.

US 60, at junction with County Route 60/ 28 (Raders Valley Road); US 60, at junction with County Route 60/41 (Old Brushy Ridge Road), Alta

UNKNOWN SOLDIERS/ GEN. LEWIS' TRACE

Six miles west, a Confederate regt. from Georgia camped at Blue Sulphur Springs in improvised shelters, during the winter of 1863. Many died of exposure and disease, and are buried on the hill 400 yards north of the spring.

Trace cleared by General Andrew Lewis on march to Point Pleasant,

This structure was built to commemorate the 1778 attack on Fort Donnally. Made of logs from the original fort, the cabin is no longer standing.

1774, from Camp Union. Campaign Bridge across Muddy Creek and the Fleshman Farm where Gen. Lee's horse "Traveller" was raised are points of interest.

WV 12, at junction with County Route 31 (Blue Sulphur Springs Road)

ALDERSON

Settled in 1777 by "Elder" John Alderson, the frontier missionary. He organized the first Baptist church in the Greenbrier Valley. In 1763, the Muddy Creek settlements were destroyed by Shawnee Indians under Cornstalk.

WV 12 (Riverview Avenue), at junction with Monroe Street, Alderson

ALDERSON BAPTIST ACADEMY AND JUNIOR COLLEGE

Alderson Academy opened September 18, 1901, a coeducational secondary school founded mainly through the efforts of Miss Emma C. Alderson. Closely associated with Greenbrier Baptist Church, after 1910 control was assumed by W.Va. Baptist Association. Designed as a home school it provided academic work in classics, sciences and normal studies. Under Dr. M.F. Forbell the Academy grew in size and number and achieved Junior College status. After 31 years as the cultural light for large neglected areas of Greenbrier and Monroe Counties the school was moved to Philippi as part of the consolidated Alderson-Broaddus College.

300 block of West Monroe Street, Alderson

RONCEVERTE

From the French word meaning "Greenbrier". Thomas Edgar settled in Greenbrier County before 1780. His son built first grist mill on Greenbrier River. Three successive mills were destroyed but the fourth plant operates today.

US 219, at junction with Locust Street, Ronceverte

PONTIAC'S WAR/ WELSH CEMETERY

Massacre of white families on Muddy Creek and of the Clendenins near here by a band of Shawnee Indians led by Chief Cornstalk, in 1763, completed the destruction of the early settlements in the Greenbrier Valley.

In this cemetery are buried pioneer settlers, including Ann (McSwain) Clendenin Rogers, the heroine of the Clendenin massacre by Shawnee Indians, July 13, 1763, and the siege of Fort Donnally in 1778, by over 200 Indians.

County Route 35 (Houfnagle Road), 1.8 miles from junction with US 60, west of Lewisburg

BIG LIME

The Greenbrier Limestone in the quarry represents the "Big Lime" of the driller. Fish-egg like oölitic zones in the "Big Lime" produce oil and natural gas in West Virginia.

US 60, just west of Lewisburg

CONFEDERATE CEMETERY/ THE CIVIL WAR

On the hill, 400 yards west, in a common grave shaped like a cross, lie unclaimed bodies of ninety-five Confederate soldiers, casualties of the area, including those of the Battle of Droop Mountain and the Battle of Lewisburg.

The Greenbrier area was predominately Southern in its sympathies, and furnished some 3000 men for the army of the Confederacy. It was occupied repeatedly by one or the other of the opposing armies throughout the War.

US 60, Library Park, Lewisburg

GREENBRIER MILITARY SCHOOL

First school was established 1808-09 by Dr. John McElhenney and chartered as an academy in 1812. Used as barracks and hospital during War between the States. The present buildings were erected in 1921.

US 219, at junction with Greenbrier Avenue, Lewisburg

GREENBRIER MILITARY SCHOOL

First established at Lewisburg 1808-09 by Dr. John McElhenney and char-

tered as an academy in 1812. Used as barracks and hospital during War between the States. Present buildings on north side of town built 1921.

US 60, between Dwyer Lane and Echols Lane, Lewisburg

LEWISBURG/LEWISBURG

Presbyterian Church established, 1783. Stone building erected, 1796, still used for worship. Lewisburg Academy founded, 1812, was precursor of Greenbrier Military School and of Greenbrier College. Library-Museum built, 1834.

Site of Fort Savannah, built in 1755. Here at Camp Union Gen. Andrew Lewis mustered troops which participated in the Battle of Point Pleasant, 1774. Lewisburg was incorporated in October, 1782, by the Virginia Assembly.

US 60, Library Park, Lewisburg

LEWISBURG BATTLE

Confederate troops under Gen. Henry Heth here, May 23, 1862, were repulsed in attack upon division of Col. Geo. Crook's brigade. The Old Stone Church was used as a hospital. In his retreat, Heth

The former Greenbrier Military School is now the home of the West Virginia School of Osteopathic Medicine. Date unknown.

burned bridge over Greenbrier at Caldwell.

US 60 (Washington Street), at junction with Lee Street, General Lewis Hotel, Lewisburg

COL. JOHN STUART/ MATHEW ARBUCKLE
Col. John Stuart built Stuart Manor, 1789, near Fort Stuart. He was a military and civil leader and led a company in the Battle of Point Pleasant. As clerk of Greenbrier County, he left many historic records. His first office is standing.

Here lived Captain Mathew Arbuckle, who guided General Andrew Lewis and army from Lewisburg to Point Pleasant and took part in the battle which followed, 1774. For a time he was in command of Fort Randolph, later built there.

US 219, at junction with Lee Street, Lewisburg

GREENBRIER COUNTY COURTHOUSE
Constructed 1837 by John W. Dunn, well known local brickmason. All brick was made locally. Building has been in constant use since its completion and is unchanged except for wings added in 1937 and 1963.

Court and Randolph streets, Courthouse Square, Lewisburg

BEREA SAND
The massive pebbly sandstone exposed in the cliff is the Berea of the driller and geologist. This sand pro-duces large quantities of oil and natural gas in West Virginia.

*US 60, 1 mile east of WV 63, near Caldwell

FRANKFORD
Col. John Stuart, who came here in 1769 with McClanahan, the Renicks, and companions, bought out earlier claims of William Hamilton. "The Cliffs" to the east offer one of the celebrated beauty spots of Greenbrier Valley.

US 219, 0.2 miles north of County Route 21 (Anthony Road), Frankford

BIG LIME
The Greenbrier Limestone, which crops out here and along U.S. Route 219 between Renick and Salt Sulphur Springs, is the "Big Lime" of the driller. Fish-egg like oölitic zones in the "Big Lime" yield oil and natural gas in West Virginia.

US 219, 0.2 miles south of County Route 9 (Friars Hill Road), south of Renick

DRY CREEK BATTLE
A two-day encounter, Aug. 26-27, 1863, between Gen. Sam Jones' Confederates and Gen. W.W. Averell's Federals. Action is also known as Howard's Creek, White Sulphur Springs and Rocky Gap. Losses: 350.

US 60, at junction with WV 92, White Sulphur Springs

KATE'S MOUNTAIN
Named for Kate Carpenter, whose husband, Nathan, was killed by the

The "Old White" in White Sulphur Springs, shown here circa 1890, was the forerunner of today's luxurious Greenbrier resort.

Indians. Fine scenic view. Home of Kate's Mountain Clover and other rare plants, such as the Box Huckleberry, 6000 years old—the oldest living thing.

US 60, at junction with County Route 60/34 (Kate Mountain Road), White Sulphur Springs

"OAKHURST" GOLF CLUB

Site of the first organized golf club in United States. It was formed, 1884, on the "Oakhurst" estate by owner, Russell W. Montague, a New Englander, and Scotchmen: George Grant, Alexander M. and Roderick McLeod and Lionel Torrin.

US 60, at junction with WV 92, White Sulphur Springs

WHITE SULPHUR/WHITE SULPHUR

Twelve Presidents, from "Old Hickory" Jackson to Woodrow Wilson, have been among the noted guests at the mineral springs where for nearly two centuries world society has made rendezvous. Shrine to General Robert E. Lee.

Large Federal fish hatcheries are located here. A mile east on Howard's Creek the armies of North and South fought in 1863. At "Oakhurst" three miles north the first golf club in America was organized in 1884.

US 60, across from the entrance to The Greenbrier, White Sulphur Springs

ORGAN CAVE

In this cave, whose beautiful natural formations have long been known, salt petre was manufactured before 1835. When war broke out between the states in 1861, it was a source of powder supply for General Lee's army.

US 219, at junction with WV 63 and County Route 62 (Hokes Mill Road)

HAMPSHIRE COUNTY

Oldest county. Authorized, 1753, in act effective, May 1, 1754. Formed from Frederick and Augusta. Lord Fairfax, owner, named it for the English shire of the same name. Ice Mountain and Hanging Rocks are among its many natural wonders.

*US 220, Hampshire-Hardy border; *WV 259, Hampshire-Hardy border; *US 50/ US 220, Hampshire-Mineral border; WV 28, Hampshire-Mineral border; *WV 9 East, Hampshire-Morgan border; *WV 9 West, Hampshire-Morgan border; *WV 127, Hampshire-Virginia border

Bloomery Iron Furnace

BLOOMERY GAP SKIRMISH/ BLOOMERY IRON FURNACE

February 14, 1862, Brigadier General Frederick W. Lander, commanding the 5th and 8th Ohio, 14th Indiana Infantry, and 400 men of the 1st West Virginia Cavalry, attacked a Confederate brigade of the 31st, 51st, 67th, and 89th Virginia Militia under Colonel J. Sencendiver. The Confederates were routed and fled toward Winchester. Lander returned to his camp at Paw Paw and Sencendiver again occupied Bloomery Gap.

The furnace was built, 1833, by Thomas Pastly and later was owned by Lewis Passmor. He placed a Mr. Cornwell in charge who operated it until 1848 when it was sold to S.A. Pancost. He and his heirs operated it until 1875 when the furnace was closed down. It was operated for a short time in 1880-1881. Annual capacity was 8500 tons. The iron was carried on rafts and flatboats down the Cacapon River.

WV 127, 2 miles east of junction with WV 29

"CAUDY'S CASTLE"

Named for James Caudy, pioneer and Indian fighter, who took refuge from the Indians on a mass of rocks overlooking Cacapon River during the French and Indian War (1754-1763). From his position on the Castle of Rocks, he defended himself by pushing the Indians, one by one with the butt of his rifle, over the precipice as they came single file along the narrow crevice of rocks. They fell 450-500 feet to the base along the edge of the Cacapon.

WV 127, 1.5 miles east of junction with WV 29

CAPON SPRINGS

Capon Springs bears Indian name meaning the "Medicine Waters." Discovered in 1765. Famous resort of early days. President Franklin Pierce, Daniel Webster, and his guest, Sir Henry Bulwer, the British Minister, were among guests.

WV 259, Capon Lake

FORT EDWARDS

Troops from this fort under Captain Mercer were ambushed in 1756 and many were killed. The French and Indians later attacked the fort but the garrison, aided by Daniel Morgan and other frontiersmen, repulsed the assault.

US 50, near junction with County Route 14 (Cacapon River Road), Capon Bridge

NORTHWESTERN TURNPIKE

In 1784, Washington proposed the Northwestern Turnpike as an all-Virginia route to the Ohio. Authorized in 1827 and started in 1831, it remains a monument to the skill of its engineers, Charles Shaw and Colonel Claudius Crozet.

US 50, Capon Bridge

ICE MOUNTAIN

Huge natural refrigerator, five miles north along North River, where ice is found for several hundred yards on the hottest summer days. Raven Rock, on North Mountain, offers one of the finest views in West Virginia.

US 50, at junction with WV 29 North

BRADDOCK'S GAP

To the north, route of General Braddock's army in May, 1755, on way to attack the French at Fort Duquesne. His troops encamped at both Fort Capon and Fort Cox near here before resuming the journey which ended in defeat and death.

US 50 and WV 29, near Pleasant Dale

ORISKANY SAND

The pure massive sandstone forming Hanging Rock is the Oriskany of the driller and geologist. The "Oriskany Sand", an important gas sand, has produced in excess of a trillion cubic feet of gas in West Virginia.

US 50, near junction with County Route 21, about 2 miles east of Pleasant Dale

ORISKANY SAND

The massive sandstone forming the top of the exposure and the great arch is the Oriskany and the limestone below it is the Helderberg of the driller and geologist. The "Oriskany Sand", an important gas sand, has produced in excess of a trillion cubic feet of gas in West Virginia.

*US 50/WV 28, about 2 miles west of Romney; *WV 28, about 1.5 miles south of Springfield*

BLUE'S GAP BATTLE

Confederate troops under Captain George F. Sheets were defeated by Colonel S.H. Dunning's 5th Ohio Infantry here, Jan. 7, 1862. North River Bridge and a number of buildings were burned by the Federals.

US 50, 14 miles east of Romney

COL. CLAUDIUS CROZET/ MECHANICSBURG GAP

Col. Crozet, born in France, 1790; came to America, 1816. He taught mathematics at West Point six years. Named chief engineer of Virginia (1824); surveyed Northwestern

Turnpike, 1825. Died 1864; buried in Shockee Hills, Richmond.

Scenic canyon cut through Mill Creek Mountain by Mill Creek. Here an old Indian trail was the pathway from the Valley of Virginia to the Alleghenies, then the Northwestern Turnpike, now the George Washington Highway.

US 50/WV 28, 2 miles west of Romney

INDIAN MOUND

The Indian Mound Cemetery, which is 7 feet high and about 15 feet in diameter, is one of the largest remaining mounds in the Eastern Panhandle of West Virginia. This mound has never been excavated but similar mounds of area dug by Smithsonian Institution suggest this mound might date between A.D. 500 and 1000, and have been constructed by Hopewellian peoples.

US 50, west end of Romney

"STONEWALL" JACKSON/ ROMNEY IN 1861-1865

Jackson arrived here Jan. 13, 1862, after capturing Bath (Berkeley Springs). Leaving Gen. Loring, he returned to Winchester. Loring's protest caused Jackson to resign but he reconsidered and his Valley Campaign followed.

Sitting astride the natural invasion route from the Shenandoah Valley to the Potomac and B. & O. Railroad, Romney was scourged by both armies. No great battles were fought here, but during the War the town changed hands 56 times.

US 50, courthouse square, Romney

ROMNEY/EARLY MEMORIAL

Incorporated as a town, 1762. Owned and laid off as a town by Lord Fairfax. Named for one of the five English Channel ports. Not far away was Fort Pearsall, built, 1756, as Indian defense. Town changed military control 56 times, 1861-1865.

In 1866, Confederate Memorial Association was formed here, which

View from courthouse square in Romney, circa late 1930s

on September 26, 1867, dedicated a monument to Confederate soldiers, one of the first erected anywhere. This was site of Indian cemetery long before white men came.

US 50, courthouse square, Romney

W. VA. SCHOOL
FOR DEAF AND BLIND

Established, 1870. The Classical Institute was donated by the Romney Literary Society as the initial building unit. Co-educational school giving academic and vocational training to the State's deaf and blind youth.

US 50, Romney

MOUNT BETHEL CHURCH

The Presbyterians established a church near here in 1792. At first called the Mountain Church in 1808, it became the nucleus of Presbyterian work in Hampshire County under the auspices of the Rev. John Lyle. The Rev. James Black reorganized the congregation in 1812 and the newly formed congregation was named Mount Bethel. The present church, built of logs in 1837, is the oldest house of worship in this county.

County Route 5 (Jersey Mountain Road), at junction with County Route 5/4 (Three Churches Hollow Road), Three Churches

FORT FORMAN

Frontier outpost. From this county, Captain William Forman (Foreman), in 1777, led a company to the relief of Fort Henry at Wheeling. He, two sons, and many others were killed in an ambush by Indians at the "Narrows" near Moundsville.

*WV 28, 3 miles north of Romney

HANGING ROCKS

Perpendicular cliffs rising nearly 300 feet above the South Branch of the Potomac. The scene of fierce battle between Delaware and Catawba Indians about 1736. Also scene of skirmishes between Northern and Southern troops in 1861.

*WV 28, 4 miles north of Romney

HIGH KNOB

This peak on Hampshire-Hardy line rises a thousand feet above the surrounding hills to a height of more than half a mile. From it can be seen points in three counties. It overlooks "The Trough", famed for its history and scenery.

US 220, near Hampshire-Hardy border

HANCOCK COUNTY

Formed in 1848 from Brooke. Named for John Hancock, first signer of the Declaration of Independence. Iron furnaces established in this county as early as 1794 made

Postcard showing Rock Spring Park, date unknown

the cannon balls that Commodore Perry used in Battle of Lake Erie.

*WV 2, Hancock-Brooke border; First Street, Weirton, Hancock-Ohio border; County Route 22/1 (Pennsylvania Avenue), Hancock-Pennsylvania border; *US 30, Hancock-Pennsylvania border*

ROCK SPRING PARK
Named for natural springs reputedly used by George Washington. Donated in 1857 for picnics and prize fights. Developed in 1897 as amusement park served by streetcar and boat attracting 15-20 thousand daily. Included dance pavilions, shooting gallerys, bowling, theatre and music hall, boating and bathing, and Scenic Railway. Automobile and changing social customs led to disuse and sale by 1970s.

WV 2 , at junction with US 30, Chester

LOGAN MASSACRE
One of the events which led up to Dunmore's War was the killing at this point of the family of Chief Logan, eloquent leader of the Mingo Indians, April, 1774, opposite their village at the mouth of Yellow Creek in Ohio.

WV 8, near junction with US 30

NEWELL
Here is located the largest single pottery unit in the world. This county has been a large producer of pottery for more than a century and today West Virginia stands second among all of the states in its production.

*WV 2, Newell

EARLY MILLS
Site of Nesselroad's powder mill which operated from 1795 to 1801.

To the south on King's Creek stood Hartford's grist mill which served local settlers in early 1800's. In 1823, Swearingen's grist mill and Eaton's saw mill were built near the same site. Nearby is the place where brothers Andrew and Adam Poe, border scouts, fought and killed Wyandott Chief Big Foot in 1781.

WV 2, at junction with County Route 66/ 2, near Moscow

NEW CUMBERLAND

Near New Cumberland, George Chapman settled, about 1783, and built an Indian fort. Here are the graves of the Chapmans, Gregorys, Graftons, and other pioneer families. Pughtown, settled about 1810, was the first county seat.

WV 2, New Cumberland

OHIO RIVER/OHIO RIVER

The river flowing past New Cumberland contributed significantly to the political, economic and social development of the town. Early settlers to New Cumberland came by river and then depended on the river as means of receiving supplies and services not produced locally.

New Cumberland was for many years an important river town, not only because of the heavy freight shipments but also as a community which supplied pilots, deck officers, engineers and crews to the many packet and tow boats on the river. The same flat boats that

brought people and supplies here became the means of expanding the fledgling clay industry.

WV 2, New Cumberland

PETER TARR FURNACE

Two miles east is the site of first blast furnace west of the Alleghenies. Built in 1794, it was the forerunner of the steel industry which flourished in this area. Here Peter Tarr cast cannon balls used by Perry on Lake Erie.

WV 2, at junction with County Route 9, Weirton

THREE SPRINGS CHURCH

100 yards south is site of original log Three Springs Church. Built 1790 on land donated by James Campbell. Elisha Macurdy, first pastor, called Nov., 1799. The mother church of Cove and Paris United Presbyterian churches.

Pennsylvania Avenue, at junction with South 17th Street, Weirton Heights, Weirton

HOLLIDAY'S COVE

East was Fort Holliday, built in 1776. During the Revolution it was a supply depot for the Continental Army. From it Col. Swearingen led troops with ammunition to relieve Fort Henry at Wheeling when attacked by Indians in 1777.

City Park, at intersection of Cove Road and Main Street, Weirton

WEIRTON

Founded, 1909, by Ernest T. Weir, industrialist. Incorporated July 1, 1947. Here is located the largest steel mill in West Virginia. Peter Tarr Furnace, among the early iron furnaces of the Alleghenies, was built here in 1794.

US 22, at junction with WV 2, Weirton

HARDY COUNTY

Formed in 1786 from Hampshire. Named for Samuel Hardy, distinguished Virginian. In 1725, John Van Meter of New York visited the South Branch Valley. He praised it highly so his sons acquired lands and settled at Old Fields.

*US 220, Hardy-Grant border; *US 220, Hardy-Hampshire border; *WV 259, Hardy-Hampshire border; WV 259, Hardy-Virginia border; *County Route 59, Hardy-Virginia border*

POPULATION CENTER

The population center of the United States was in present West Virginia four times as it moved westward across the nation: near Wardensville in 1820; at Smoke Hole in 1830; west of Buckhannon in 1840; near Burning Springs in 1850.

WV 55, east of Wardensville

TUSCARORA (CLINTON) SAND

The massive resistant Tuscarora Sandstone is nearly vertical here and forms the top of the great arch of Hanging Rock Gap. The "Tuscarora (Clinton) Sand" pro-

Wardensville, date unknown

duces some gas, although it is largely unexplored in West Virginia.

WV 55, near Wardensville

WARDENSVILLE

George Washington laid off land here for William Wallace Warden, Nov. 11, 1749. Warden built a stockade fort, near which members of his family were killed by Indians, 1758, and the fort burned. Scene of skirmishes in 1862-1863.

WV 259/WV 55, Wardensville

LOST AND FOUND

Here Lost River disappears under Sandy Ridge. Two miles away on the other side of the mountain the stream is "found" again as the headwaters of the Cacapon River. This stream has the Indian name for "Medicine Waters".

WV 259, near Wardensville

ORISKANY SAND

The massive sandstone forming the cliff is the Oriskany of the driller, and the geologist. The "Oriskany Sand", an important gas sand, has produced in excess of a trillion cubic feet of gas in West Virginia.

WV 259/WV 55, just east of junction with WV 29

LOST RIVER

Settled before 1750. Near by was Riddle's Fort, frontier outpost. Here Battle of Lost River was fought in 1756 between company of Virginia frontiersmen under Captain Jeremiah Smith and band of 50 French and Indians.

WV 259, Lost River

LOST RIVER'S FIRST CHURCH

300 yards east is the first Lost River Valley Church. Built of logs, prior to 1797, on land deeded by Anthony Miller, 1831, to the Baptists and Presbyterians "to hold in common for a meetinghouse and graveyard."

WV 259, Lost City

HOWARD'S LICK/JACKSON HOME

Howard's Lick, (3 Mi. W.), or Lee

White Sulphur Springs, was once owned by Gen. Henry "Light Horse Harry" Lee of Revolutionary War fame. It was owned later by Charles Carter Lee, brother of the beloved Gen. Robert E. Lee.

Here John Jackson and wife, great-grandparents of Gen. "Stonewall" Jackson, settled about 1750 and here was born Edward Jackson, grandfather of the great military genius, before the family moved to the Buckhannon River.

WV 259, just north of Mathias

MT. OLIVE LUTHERAN CHURCH

Founded in 1888 by Dr. Conrad B. Gohdes last of the Lutheran horseback circuit riders, who was known as a dynamic pastor, theologian, professor of history, philologist and a Christian gentleman. Died 1952 A.D.

County Route 7, just north of Peru Community Bridge

The frame-and-log cabin on the right was built circa 1800 as a summer retreat and hunting lodge by General Henry "Lighthorse Harry" Lee, father of Robert E. Lee. The restored cabin is now part of Lost River State Park.

Built in the late 1700s on the site of the original log home and fortress, and shown here in the late 1800s, "Fort Pleasant" is situated above "the Trough," a natural feature along the South Branch of the Potomac.

FORT PLEASANT
Built on lands of Isaac Van Meter who took up claim near Old Fields, 1735, and settled there, 1744. In chain of forts which Washington established. For a time it was garrisoned by British regulars. Near it was Battle of the Trough, 1756.

US 220, 4 miles north of Moorefield, Old Fields

MOOREFIELD
Chartered, 1777, and named for Conrad Moore, early settler. During Indian wars, Town Fort, north, and Fort Buttermilk, south, gave protection. Here, 1794, Gen. Biggs brought part of the troops re-cruited to suppress Whisky Rebellion.

US 220, at junction with WV 55 East, Moorefield

GEN. JOSEPH NEVILLE/ MCNEILL'S RAID
Near here, grave of Gen. Joseph Neville; officer in Revolution; member of conventions of 1775 and 1776. With Alexander McLean of Pennsylvania, he completed survey of Mason and Dixon Line in 1782. His son, Joseph, was a major general in War of 1812.

Here, 1865, McNeill's Rangers under Lieut. Jesse C. McNeill started raid on Cumberland where they captured Generals Kelley and Crook of the Union Army. The Rangers, organized by Capt. John Hanson McNeil, performed many daring deeds.

US 220/WV 28, Moorefield

HARRISON COUNTY

Formed, 1784, from Monongalia. It included all or parts of 17 other counties. Named for Benjamin Harrison, signer of Declaration of Independence and the governor of Virginia, 1781-84. Birthplace of Thomas J. "Stonewall" Jackson.

*WV 57, Harrison-Barbour border; WV 20, Harrison-Barbour border; *US 50, Harrison-Doddridge border; WV 23, Harrison-Doddridge border; US 19, Harrison-Lewis border; *US 19, Harrison-Marion border; *County Route 73, Harrrison-Taylor border; *US 50, Harrison-Taylor border; WV 76, Harrison-Taylor border; *WV 20, Harrison-Wetzel border*

ENTERPRISE

Nearby is the McIntire blockhouse, built in 1773, another of the outposts established as protection against the Indians. Here are the graves of many early settlers, including those of John McIntire and wife, both victims of the Indians.

US 19, Enterprise

REVOLUTIONARY GRAVES

On the opposite (east) side of the West Fork River, in the Enterprise I.O.O.F. Cemetery, are the graves of Jacob Bigler (1752-1829) and Elisha Griffith(1751-1840), Revolutionary War veterans from Maryland who settled in Harrison Co. after the war. The graves are marked by a monument erected in 1933 by Daniel Davisson Chapter of the Daughters of the American Revolution.

US 19, Enterprise

LEVI SHINN HOUSE

Built, 1778, by Levi Shinn who came from New Jersey, 1773, and claimed tomahawk rights. Returned with family and brothers, Clement and Jonathan and settled. Sold part of land to Jonathan whose son, Levi, deeded it for site of Shinnston.

US 19, Shinnston

LUMBERPORT

Near blockhouse built by Thomas Harbert and others about 1775. This was the home of Colonel Benjamin Robinson who was a soldier in the Revolution. He led a company at Brandywine and Germantown and also saw Indian service.

WV 20, Lumberport

SALTWELL

Village so named because of well drilled here in 1835 by Abraham and Peter Righter. The well reached a depth of 745 feet releasing natural gas. Often attributed to be first deep well drilled in United States. Water from such wells was reputed to have medicinal value. Some salt was produced here but these efforts were abandoned as Kanawha Valley production and influence increased.

WV 131, 3.3 miles south of junction with US 19, Saltwell

SIMPSON CREEK COVERED BRIDGE

A.S. Hugill built 75' long by 14' wide multiple king-post truss bridge in 1881 for $1483 on land of John Lowe. Survived great flood of 1888 but was washed away from original site 1/2 mile upstream in 1899.

County Route 24/7 (Despard-Summit Park Road), near junction with County Route 24, Bridgeport

JOHN POWERS' FORT

On Simpson Creek is site of fort built by John Powers, 1771. Nearby is grave of Col. Benjamin Wilson, soldier and settler. Here lived Joseph Johnson, only Virginia governor from west of Alleghenies; first elected by popular vote.

US 50, Bridgeport

**Virginia Governor
Joseph Johnson (1785-1877)**

"RANDOLPH MASON"

Near by was the home of the late Melville Davisson Post, author of many novels, but particularly noted for his stories concerning the strange points of law, woven about the fictitious character "Randolph Mason".

*WV 20, 9 miles south of Clarksburg, Romine's Mill

B&O DEPOT

Built 1892, following the completion of railroad in 1887. Lost Creek grew to become largest shipping point for cattle in West Virginia in 1915 and on entire B&O system, east of Mississippi in 1923.

County Route 48 (Johnstown Road), at junction with Railroad Street, Lost Creek

WEST MILLFORD

Site of Richards' Fort or Lowther's Fort. Colonel William Lowther settled near, 1772, served under George Rogers Clark, and was colonel of the northwestern counties of Virginia. Near by Indians killed the Richards and Washburns.

US 19, at junction with WV 270 East, West Milford

NUTTER'S FORT

Built by Thomas Nutter in 1772 after settlement two years earlier. Nutter was a captain in the Revolutionary Army and is buried here. Refugees from Hacker's Creek settlements came here during the Indian raids of 1779.

WV20, Nutter Fort

CENTER BRANCH CHURCH

Organized in 1818 by 19 members of Simpson Creek Baptist Church wanting a house of worship nearer to their homes. Original log building stood below road. Present structure was erected in 1854.

WV 20, 0.3 miles north of WV 58, Nutter Fort

OAK MOUNDS

Directly to the east are two earthen, domed burial mounds. The larger mound is some sixty feet in diameter and twelve feet high. Excavations in 1969 revealed flint tools, pottery sherds and skeletal remains of two individuals. Site dates to about 100 BC, late Early Woodland Period.

WV 98, 0.5 miles off US 19 near Veterans Hospital, Clarksburg

OAK MOUNDS

On the crown of the hill to the east is a large Indian mound and to the west of it is a smaller mound. These mounds have never been excavated but they were probably built by the Hopewellian culture between A.D. 1 and 1000. The larger mound is about 12 feet high and 60 feet in diameter. A number of burials of important persons of the culture probably occur in these mounds.

US 19, at junction with County Route 19/ 57 (Armory Road), Clarksburg

CLARKSBURG/CLARKSBURG

Established, 1785. Named for Gen. George Rogers Clark. John Simpson camped here in 1764. Early perma-

nent settlements were made by the Davissons, Cottrills, Sotha Hickman, Nicholas Carpenter, and others.

Site of Randolph Academy, 1785. Home of Gen. Nathan Goff and John S. Carlile. Supply depot of the Union Army, 1861 to 1865. General George B. McClellan had his headquarters here in 1861 until Battle of Bull Run.

West Main Street, at junction with South Third Street, courthouse square, Clarksburg

"STONEWALL" JACKSON

Birthplace of General Thomas J. "Stonewall" Jackson. After a brilliant Mexican War record, he joined the Confederacy in 1861, earned his nickname and advancement in rank in first Battle of Bull Run, and was killed at Chancellorsville.

West Main Street, at junction with South Third Street, Clarksburg

THE JACKSON CEMETERY

In this cemetery lie buried members of the Stonewall Jackson family: his father Jonathan, a sister Elizabeth, his great grandparents John Jackson

General "Stonewall" Jackson's Clarksburg birthplace is shown in this postcard, date unknown.

and wife Elizabeth Cummings. Buried here also are Mrs. Mary Payne Jackson and Mrs. Mary Coles Payne, sister and mother of Dorothy (Dolly) Madison, wife of President James Madison. Some Civil War soldiers lie buried in this place; called Jackson Park.

WV 20 (East Pike Street), near junction with US 50, Clarksburg

JOHN SIMPSON

In 1764, John Simpson, hunter and trapper, established a camp here on the bank of the West Fork River opposite the mouth of Elk Creek. He was the first white man in the area. Simpson Creek and town of Simpson are named for him.

US 19 split, Clarksburg

VETERANS ADMINISTRATION HOSPITAL

A 212-bed general medical and surgical hospital, dedicated Dec. 17, 1950 and activated for patients in March 1951. It maintains 97 medical, 90 surgical and 25 psychiatric beds. It is affiliated with the West Virginia University School of Medicine.

WV 98, Clarksburg

TOWERS SCHOOL

Built in 1894 and named in honor of Reverend George Towers, graduate of Oxford, England who was a teacher at Randolph Academy. The Academy, authorized by the Virginia Assembly in 1787, stood just to the east and was the principal regional school from 1795 to 1843. The Northwestern Virginia Academy, incorporated by the Virginia Legislature in 1842, occupied this site from 1843-1893.

*200 Hewes Avenue, Clarksburg

SALEM

Chartered, 1794, and settled by colony of families from New Jersey. Site of blockhouse where troops were stationed during Indian wars to guard the trail from the Ohio to the West Fork settlements. It is seat of Salem College.

100 block of West Main Street, Salem

INDUSTRIAL HOME FOR GIRLS

The West Virginia Industrial Home for Girls was established by act of the Legislature, February 18, 1897, for the rehabilitation of girls who need assistance in becoming useful citizens of the State. It was formally opened May 5, 1899.

West Main Street, near junction with County Route 38 (Long Run Road), Salem

JACKSON COUNTY

Formed in 1831 from Kanawha, Mason, and Wood. Named for General Andrew Jackson, the seventh President of the United States. Jesse Hughes, noted Indian fighter, spent his declining years in the county where he is buried.

County Route 21, Jackson-Kanawha border; *US 33, Jackson-Mason border; WV 2, Jackson-Mason border; WV 34, Jackson-Putnam border; US 33, Jackson-Roane border; County Route 21, Jackson-Wirt border; *WV 68, Jackson-Wood border

Railroad magnate Henry G. Davis donated $50,000 toward construction of the West Virginia Industrial Home for Girls. The school, which opened near Salem in 1899, is now part of the West Virginia Division of Juvenile Services. Date unknown.

John Edward Kenna

KENNA

Post office established here July 1, 1880, with Grandville P. Morrison as first postmaster. Named in honor of John Edward Kenna (1848-1893), member of the U.S. House of Representatives (1879-1883), and later elected to the U.S. Senate (1883-93). O.J. Morrison, son of Grandville Morrison, opened first O.J. Morrison store here in 1890. Evolved into a statewide chain of locally managed department stores.

*WV 34, 0.8 miles west of junction with I-77, Kenna

STAATS MILL COVERED BRIDGE

Built in 1887 over Tug Fork of Mill Creek and named for Enoch Staats' mill. Jackson Co. Court paid local builder H.T. Hartley $904 to erect "Long" truss wooden superstructure. Total cost of original 97 ft. bridge with stone abutments and approaches was $1724. Removed from Staats Mill and restored to original specifications on new abutments at this site in 1983 cost in excess of $104,000.

County Route 25, Cedar Lakes FFA-FHA State Camp, east of Ripley

RIPLEY

Established in 1832 on land which was settled by William John and Lewis Rogers in 1768 and later acquired by Jacob and Ann (Staats) Starcher. Near here lived Capt. Wil-

View of Ripley, circa 1910

liam Parsons who was active in the early life of Jackson County.

County Route 21, 1 block from junction with US 33, Ripley

COTTAGEVILLE
Michael Coleman, member of a hunting party from frontier fort at Belleville, was killed and scalped by the Indians at this point about 1793. Near by at Mill Creek falls, Benjamin Wright built an early power flour mill.

US 33, Millsite Park, Cottageville

WASHINGTON'S LAND
Westward lies the Millwood Tract of 4,395 acres patented by George Washington on December 15, 1772, based on a survey made in June 1771. It bordered on the Ohio River above the Great Bend for "five miles and 700 poles."

*WV 2 at Pleasant View overlook, 4 miles south of Ravenswood

OHIO RIVER FORD/RAVENSWOOD
Sand Creek Riffle, where the Indians and pioneers crossed the Ohio, was used by General Jenkins when he carried the Confederate flag into Ohio in 1862, and also by the Union Army under General Lightburn in its retreat the same year.

These lands were surveyed, 1771, for George Washington by Colonel William Crawford, who later was taken captive by the Indians and burned at the stake. Washington camped near in 1770. Here is grave of Jesse Hughes, noted scout.

WV 2, Washington Lands, Western Waters Museum, Ravenswood

JEFFERSON COUNTY
Formed in 1801 from Berkeley. Named for Thomas Jefferson. Home of Generals Gates, Darke, and Charles Lee. Here four companies of Washington's men organized. Shepherdstown was strongly urged as the seat of the National Capitol.

WV 51, Jefferson-Berkeley border; *WV 9, Jefferson-Berkeley border; *WV 45, Jefferson-Berkeley border; WV 9, Jefferson-Virginia border; US 340 North, Jefferson-Virginia border

KEYES GAP
Formerly Vestal's Gap. Historic gateway through the Blue Ridge into the Shenandoah Valley. In 1755, part of Braddock's army passed here en route to Fort Duquesne. It was often used by Washington, and by armies of the Blue and the Gray, 1861-65.

WV 9, near Jefferson-Virginia border

IRON FURNACES
Thomas Mayberry agreed in 1742 to erect iron furnaces on the property of William Vestal. Here ore was mined and iron produced for the first time west of the Blue Ridge. Washington visited the iron furnaces here in 1760.

*WV 9, at Bloomery, approximately 4 miles east of Charles Town

The U.S. armory and arsenal complex at Harpers Ferry, shown here in 1861, was the scene of John Brown's famous 1859 raid. Brown was captured in the armory's engine house, pictured at left. The building is now part of the Harpers Ferry National Historical Park.

HARPERS FERRY/ JOHN BROWN'S FORT

Named for Robert Harper, who settled here, 1734. Scene of raid by John Brown in 1859 to seize the Federal arsenal and armory built here, 1796. He was captured by U.S. troops under Colonel Robert E. Lee, convicted of treason and hanged.

The United States building in which John Brown and his companions were captured was exhibited at the Chicago World's Fair in 1893, and now is on campus of Storer College above the town. This school, established, 1866, was one of the first Negro colleges.

US 340, Washington and Jackson streets, Harpers Ferry

PRIZE OF WAR

Harpers Ferry was much sought by North and South, 1861-1865. Its garrison of 12,000 Union troops was captured by army of Gen. "Stonewall" Jackson, Sept. 15, 1862, on way to join Lee at Antietam. The Catholic Church was used as Federal hospital.

US 340, Washington Street, Harpers Ferry

UNION SKIRMISH LINE

Harpers Ferry was much sought by North and South, 1861-1865. Its garrison of 12,000 Union troops was captured by army of Gen. "Stonewall" Jackson, Sept. 15, 1862, on way to join Lee at Antietam. The Catholic Church was used as Federal hospital.

County Route 27, near junction with US 340, Harpers Ferry

"BEALLAIR"

Colonel Lewis Washington, who lived here, was one of the hostages captured by John Brown in 1859 in his raid on Harpers Ferry. When captured, Brown wore a sword, once owned by George Washington, taken from this home. (1 Mi. N.)

US 340 and WV 230, Halltown

GENERAL WILLIAM DARKE

Within these grounds is the home of General William Darke (1736-1801), who served as officer in American Revolution and in St. Clair's 1791 expedition against Miami Indians in Ohio. He served as delegate to the Virginia Convention called in 1788 to ratify the Federal Constitution, was elected to the Va. Assembly of 1791, and was an original trustee for the town of Charles Town.

County routes 17 and 17/2, at intersection with railroad tracks, Duffields

PACK HORSE FORD

Early settlers crossed the Potomac here. "Stonewall" Jackson and A.P. Hill used ford enroute to Battle of Antietam. Here Lee's army forded after battle with the Corn Exchange

Regiment & other Federals in pursuit.

County Route 17/1, 1 mile east of Shepherdstown

THE JAMES RUMSEY BRIDGE

Named in honor of the inventor, James Rumsey, who made successful public demonstrations of his steamboat on the Potomac River here on December 3 and 11, 1787. Opened and dedicated on July 15, 1939.

WV 480, Jefferson-Maryland border

SHEPHERD STATE TEACHERS COLLEGE

Established in 1872 as a branch of State normal school system. It was an outgrowth of the old Shepherd College. This is the site of early settlement made by Thomas Shepherd who built a fort here during Indian days.

Junction of German and North King streets, Shepherdstown

SHEPHERDSTOWN

James Rumsey, inventor of the steamboat, lived here, 1785 to 1788, and in 1787 demonstrated his boat on the Potomac at this point. Here was born Colonel James Strode Swearingen, who commanded the men who founded the City of Chicago in 1803.

*WV 480, Shepherdstown

SHEPHERDSTOWN/ SHEPHERDSTOWN

Oldest town in West Virginia. Early settlers, 1707-1732, crossed Pack Horse Ford one mile east. Founded by Thomas Shepherd in 1762. Here lived James Rumsey, inventor of steamboat. First company of Southern Soldiers to join Washington at Boston met at spring south of town. Shepherd College founded 1872.

Once Mecklenberg. Settlements about 1719. Named for Thomas Shepherd, its founder, and incorporated in 1762. First church (Presbyterian), west of the Blue Ridge was here. First W.Va. newspaper, 1790. First W.Va. post office, 1792.

WV 480, Shepherdstown

SHEPHERD COLLEGE

Incorporated as Shepherd College, 1871. Chartered by act of the Legislature, Feb. 27, 1872, as the Shepherd College State Normal School. Name changed in 1931 to Shepherd State Teachers College and in 1943, to Shepherd College.

WV 480, Shepherdstown

"TRAVELERS' REST"

Home of Gen. Horatio Gates, built on land bought, 1763. Gates, once a British officer, joined the Revolutionary Army, and was the leader of the Continentals in decisive victory over Gen. Burgoyne at Saratoga. (1/2 Mi. S. W.).

WV 9/WV 480, Kearneysville

"THE BOWER"

Three miles west, on Opequon Creek, lived General Adam Stephen, 1754-1772. Original tract, with hunting lodge, was bought in 1750. The present mansion was built by Adam Stephen Dandridge, his grandson, in 1805.

County Route 3 (Paynes Ford Road) and County Route 1, near Leetown

"PRATO RIO"

Home of General Charles Lee, built on land bought in 1774. Lee, colonel in British army, resigned his commission and joined the colonists after Battle of Lexington. On this estate, the U.S. Government maintains a fish hatchery.

County Route 1, between Kearneysville and Middleway

CAMERON'S DEPOT

Here, August 21, 1864, General Philip H. Sheridan's Federal forces were defeated by General Jubal A. Early. The fighting swept over such fine old estates as Harewood, Sulgrave, Tuscawillow, Cedar Lawn, and Locust Hill, still marked by shot and shell.

WV 51, 5 miles west of Charles Town

CEDAR LAWN

1 1/2 mi. S is 1825 home of John T.A. Washington, a great nephew of the 1st president. Land part of "Harewood" plot of Sam'l Washington, a brother of George. Original site of 1780 home "Berry Hill."

WV 51 and O'Sullivan Road, 3.5 miles west of Charles Town

RICHWOOD HALL
The original brick house was built on land owned by Lawrence Augustine Washington, the son of Samuel Washington, George's brother. The present mansion-house, in an excellent state of preservation, was built about 1825. During the Battle of Cameron's Depot, Aug. 21, 1864, Confederate General Jubal A. Early placed his cannon near the house and formed his battle lines north and south of this point.

County Route 51/1 (Earl or O'Sullivan Road), 0.8 miles southeast of WV 51

"HAREWOOD"
Home of Colonel Samuel Washington, brother of General Washington.

Built about 1770. Mantelpiece given by Lafayette. Among its guests, Louis Philippe, later King of France. Here Dolly Payne Todd and James Madison, later President, were married.

WV 51, west of Charles Town

"LOCUST HILL"
Half mile southwest is the mansion built by John B. and Lucy Washington Packette in 1840. Center of conflict between Generals Early and Sheridan in 1864. It still shows marks of their musket firing and cannonading.

*WV 51, 3 miles west of Charles Town

RUINS OF ST. GEORGE'S CHAPEL
This chapel was built by devout people of (then) Frederick Parish, Frederick County, Virginia who

The ruins of St. George's Chapel. Built near Charles Town in the late 1760s, the structure served as the area's Episcopal church until the Zion Episcopal Church was constructed in 1817.

joined Col. Robert Worthington in completing it in 1769. It was first called the English Church, then Berkeley Church, then Norborne Chapel, as the parish was Norborne, 1770-1815. The Rev. Daniel Sturgis was its first minister of record, 1771-1785. The Washington, Nourse, Davenport and Throckmorton families worshipped here.

WV 51, west of Charles Town

PIEDMONT

Robert Worthington settled here in 1730 and built stone house called "Quarry Bank" after his family home in England. Son Robert Jr. helped establish nearby St. George's Chapel in 1769. James Nourse bought tract, known as "Piedmont," in 1770, and deeded it in 1786 to John Briscoe, who added present brick mansion to stone kitchen. It remained in family until 1979 death of Louise Briscoe.

WV 51, 2 miles west of Charles Town

WASHINGTON'S LAND

The "Bullskin" or Rock Hall Tract, the first land owned by George Washington in West Virginia, was surveyed by him, Nov. 24, 1750. Bought from Captain Rutherford, it became a part of Washington's 2,233-acre tract in this area.

County Route 13 (Summit Point Road), west of Charles Town

"CLAYMONT COURT"

Bushrod Corbin Washington, grandnephew of General George Washington, built this home in 1820. It was destroyed by fire, 1838, and rebuilt. Later it was the home of Frank R. Stockton, novelist, who here wrote his last book. (2 Mi. SW)

WV 51 and County Route 13 (Summit Point Road), west of Charles Town

"BLAKELEY"

Home of General Washington's grandnephew, John Augustine Washington, who later became the

George Washington's great-nephew built "Blakeley" shortly before inheriting Mount Vernon.

The Jefferson County Courthouse in Charles Town was the site of two famous treason trials–that of John Brown in 1859 for his raid on the federal arsenal at Harpers Ferry and that of Bill Blizzard for his role in the 1921 armed miners' march on Logan County.

owner of Mount Vernon. "Blakeley", built about 1820, was partially burned a few years later and then rebuilt in its present form. (1 1/2 Mi. W.)

Huyett Road, 0.2 miles west of junction with old US 340 (US 340 bypass), near Charles Town

CHARLES TOWN
Founded in 1786 by Charles Washington, brother of the President. Here John Brown was tried and convicted of treason. Home of W.L. Wilson, Postmaster General, 1896, who here started the first rural free delivery in America.

US 340, at junction with WV 9, at courthouse, Charles Town

HAPPY RETREAT
Now called Mordington. Home of Colonel Charles Washington, founder of Charles Town, Virginia (now West Virginia). His brother General George Washington often visited him here. Colonel Washington died in September 1799. He and his wife Mildred are buried on the estate.

WV 9, Charles Town

FREEDOM'S CALL
Grave of Robert Rutherford, member of committee which in 1775 replied to orders of Lord Dunmore for Virginians to join British army or be held as rebels. This defiance was a gauntlet hurled at Dunmore's feet. (1 1/2 Mi. N. E.)

US 340, east of Charles Town; US 340, approximately 0.5 miles east of Charles Town

PETER BURR HOUSE
Built in 1751 by Peter Burr, cousin of Aaron Burr, on a grant of 480 acres from Lord Fairfax. The house is one of the state's oldest frame structures. It is a fine example of a mid-18th century Virginia family homestead which traces its origins to English yeoman home construction of the Elizabethan period. Sold in 1798 by Peter's son, the house was repurchased by the family in 1878.

WV 9, at junction with West Burr Boulevard, approximately 3 miles north of Charles Town

KANAWHA COUNTY
Authorized, 1788; organized in 1789 from Greenbrier and Montgomery. Named for the Kanawha River, bearing name of Indian tribe. Salt making brought early settlers into the valley and from it grew vast modern chemical plants.

*US 119, Kanawha-Boone border; WV 94, Kanawha-Boone border; *WV 4, Kanawha-Clay border; WV 61, Kanawha-Fayette border; US 60, Kanawha-Fayette border; County Route 21, Kanawha-Jackson border; *WV 214, Kanawha-Lincoln border; US 35, Kanawha-Putnam border; *WV 25, Kanawha-Putnam border; *US 60, Kanawha-Putnam border; WV 62, Kanawha-Putnam border; *US 119, Kanawha-Roane border

PRATT

First settled in early 1780s and incorporated in 1905. Important site in 1912-13 Paint-Cabin Creek Strike. Labor organizer "Mother Jones" spent her 84th birthday imprisoned here. Pratt Historic District, listed on the National Register in 1984, recognizes the town's important residential architecture from early plantation to Victorian styles.

WV 61, Pratt

ANDREW & CHARLES LEWIS MARCH

The nearby highway is part of route traversing W.Va. from Lewisburg to Point Pleasant memorialized by the state to commemorate the march of the American Colonial army of 1,200 men led by Andrew & Charles Lewis. After a month's march this army defeated a Shawnee Indian force led by Cornstalk at the Battle of Point Pleasant on the banks of the Ohio & Kanawha rivers, October 10, 1774.

US 60 East and County Route 81 (Kellys Creek Road) at church, Cedar Grove; WV 25, Shawnee Park, West Dunbar

FIRST SETTLERS

Walter Kelly settled here about 1773 but was killed by Indians. William Morris came here in 1774 and made first permanent settlement in this valley. He built a fort, had a "boat yard," and started a church and school.

US 60 East and County Route 81 (Kellys Creek Road) at church, Cedar Grove

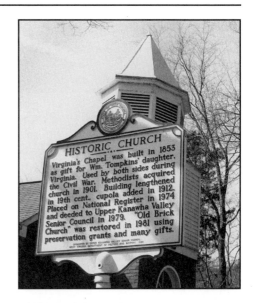

HISTORIC CHURCH

Virginia's Chapel was built in 1853 as gift for Wm. Tompkins' daughter, Virginia. Used by both sides during the Civil War, Methodists acquired church in 1901. Building lengthened in 19th cent., cupola added in 1912. Placed on National Register in 1974 and deeded to Upper Kanawha Valley Senior Council in 1979. "Old Brick Church" was restored in 1981 using preservation grants and many gifts.

US 60 East and County Route 81 (Kellys Creek Road) at church, Cedar Grove

COALBURG

Here was the home of W.H. Edwards, naturalist and explorer, who led an important expedition to the Amazon in 1846 and was one of the chief authorities on butterflies and moths. He was a descendant of renowned Jonathan Edwards.

US 60 East, 2.2 miles west of Cedar Grove

SAMUEL SHREWSBURY HOUSE

House built circa 1810 by Samuel Shrewsbury (1763-1835) on a 704 acre tract of land received from Colonel John Dickinson. Sandstone and hewn hardwood logs used in construction were obtained locally from the land. Shrewsbury, a revolutionary soldier, and his family, moved here in 1798 from Bedford County, Virginia. He and his brother John became active with Dickinson in the salt industry.

US 60, Belle

BURNING SPRINGS

Here in 1773 the Van Bibbers and others found gas bubbling through waters of a spring, which, much to their surprise, ignited. Two years later, this tract of land was patented by George Washington and General Andrew Lewis.

US 60, Belle

CAMP PIATT

Civil War camp named for Col. Abraham Piatt, Ohio Zouaves. Its strategic location on the James River & Kanawha Turnpike and the Kanawha River aided Union troops guarding the Kanawha Valley and patrolling western Virginia. Future U.S. presidents, Rutherford Hayes and William McKinley of the 23rd Ohio, were stationed here in 1863.

US 60, West Belle

REV. RUFFNER'S GRAVE

In cemetery nearby is grave of Dr. Henry Ruffner, eminent theologian and writer, called father of Presbyterianism in the Kanawha region. After his ministry, he became head of Washington College, Lexington, Va. Wrote Ruffner Pamphlet.

*US 60, between Malden and Charleston

RUFFNER WELL

In 1808 David and Joseph Ruffner near here on the bank of the Kanawha completed a well into solid rock to a depth of 59 feet by a method and with drilling tools they devised, which was further developed in this valley by themselves and Billye Morris into what is now known as the cable tool method of drilling. Drilling tools and drillers from the Kanawha Valley drilled the first well for oil at Titusville, Pennsylvania.

US 60, Malden

MALDEN/BOOKER T. WASHINGTON HOMEPLACE

Early salt-making industry that was centered here peaked in the 1850s. In 1755, Mary Ingles and Betty Draper made salt for their Indian captors here at "Buffalo Salt Licks." John Dickinson bought the site in 1785. Wells sunk by Brooks and Ruffners in early 1800s led to thriving salt and related industries. Site of African Zion Baptist Church, the state's black Baptist mother church, placed on National Register of Historic Places, 1980.

Washington, born in a slave cabin in Hales Ford, VA, ca. 1856, spent

Booker T. Washington, left, is shown here, circa 1910, with prominent West Virginia education leaders Byrd Prillerman, center, and Kelly Miller.

his early childhood in Kanawha Salines, now Malden, where he worked days in the salt industry and attended school for blacks at night. Upon his graduation from Hampton Institute, he returned to teach public and Sunday school for two years. Later, as Tuskegee Institute president, he often visited his half sister Amanda Johnson here.

US 60, Malden

DANIEL BOONE
Across the Great Kanawha River, lived Daniel Boone, the noted frontiersman, from about 1788 to 1795. He represented Kanawha County in the Virginia Assembly, 1791; was Lieut. Col. of Virginia militia during Indian wars.

US 60, Daniel Boone Park, Charleston

CRAIK-PATTON HOUSE
Built 1834 as "Elm Grove" by James Craik, grandson of Geo. Washington's personal physician. Sold to George Smith Patton, 1858, and retained by family until end of Civil War. Born here was father of noted World War II general Geo. S. Patton. Moved to Lee St. from original Virginia St. location in 1906. Acquired by City of Charleston in 1968 and leased to Colonial Dames. Moved to park 1973.

US 60, near Daniel Boone Park, Charleston

LEWIS' MARCH
Near this place, the army of Gen. Andrew Lewis camped, Sept. 21, 1774, enroute from Lewisburg. From

Charleston, Lewis led his men by land and water to Point Pleasant where Cornstalk's Indians were defeated, Oct. 10, 1774.

US 60 (Kanawha Boulevard), at junction with Veazey Street, Charleston

STATE CAPITOL
Constructed of buff Indiana limestone and lined with Imperial Danby marble from Vermont, the State's Capitol is considered one of the world's superb examples of Italian Renaissance architecture. Designed by the internationally prominent Cass Gilbert and dedicated on June 20, 1932 by Governor William G. Conley as "a monument to West Virginians of yesterday, today and tomorrow", this magnificent Capitol cost $10,000,000.

Greenbrier Street, at junction with Washington Street East, Capitol Complex, Charleston

STATE CAPITOL
West Virginia's Capitol first located in Wheeling, 1863; moved to Charleston, 1870; back to Wheeling, 1875; and finally to Charleston, 1885. It was located two miles west until destroyed by fire, 1921. Present building was completed in 1931.

US 60 East (Kanawha Boulevard), across from State Capitol, Charleston

STATE CAPITOL
West Virginia's Capitol first located in Wheeling, 1863; located in Charleston, 1870; again in Wheeling, 1875, and finally in Charleston, 1885.

It was located 2 mi. west until destroyed by fire, 1921. Present building was completed in 1932.

US 60 (Kanawha Boulevard), at junction with Greenbrier Street, Holly Grove mansion, Charleston

EXECUTIVE MANSION

In 1924, ground was broken for this magnificent Georgian colonial style mansion, official home of the State's governors since 1926. Designed by W.F. Martens, it was constructed of colonial Harvard brick at an initial cost of $203,000.

US 60 East (Kanawha Boulevard), near junction with Greenbrier Street, Charleston

THE RUFFNERS

Grave of Joseph Ruffner, who bought the site of Charleston from the Clendenins. His son, Daniel, built Holly Mansion on Kanawha Street in 1815. The Ruffners aided oil and gas development by improved drills used in salt wells.

US 60 East (Kanawha Boulevard), Charleston

FIRST GAS WELL

In 1815 Captain James Wilson while drilling here for salt brine vowed he would drill to Hades if necessary. A large flow of gas was struck that ignited and burned with a huge flame, apparently fulfilling the captain's original vow.

US 60 East (Kanawha Boulevard), at junction with Brooks Street, Charleston

CHARLESTON

Founded by George Clendenin and named for his father. Established, 1794. Fort Lee, built, 1788, stood on Kanawha River. "Mad Anne" Bailey, the border heroine, and Daniel Boone and Simon Kenton, noted scouts, once lived here.

*US 60 East (Kanawha Boulevard), Courthouse, Charleston

STATE CAPITOL

West Virginia's Capitol is much traveled; Wheeling to Charleston to Wheeling and then back to Charleston, it moved. At this spot it stood from 1885 until destroyed by fire in 1921. The Capitol now stands two miles east.

Lee Street, at junction with Capitol Street, Charleston

FORT LEE

A western frontier outpost, guarding settlers against the Indians. Built here in 1788 and named for Gen. Henry "Light Horse Harry" Lee, one of Washington's most trusted officers. Later Lee was governor of Virginia.

US 60 East (Kanawha Boulevard), near junction with Brooks Street, Charleston

FORT SCAMMON

At the top of the hill is the site of an earthwork fort built by Union soldiers in 1863. During the battle of Sept. 13, 1862, Confederate artillery fired on Charleston from this place. Hayes and McKinley, future presidents, served at the fort.

Fort Hill Drive, just off US 119, Charleston

SIMON KENTON

Simon Kenton, the hero of the Virginia and Kentucky borders, with George Strader and John Yeager, camped on Elk River, 1771-73. Attacked by Indians, Yeager was killed, but Kenton and Strader, although wounded, made their escape.

US 119, 0.5 miles north of junction with WV 114, Big Chimney

PINCH REUNION

Oldest of its kind in nation. Founded in 1902 by William W. Wertz and other Elk River residents to raise the civic, religious and educational standards of the community. The group meets for three days every August at its home site, "Rockwood Glen." Prominent speakers appear on the programs. The Pinch schoolhouse (1865-1913) on the grounds was acquired by the Association and is now used as a community building.

County Route 47, 1 mile north of junction with County Route 49, Reunion Park, Pinch

CAPTAIN JOHN YOUNG/ JOHN YOUNG EARLY SETTLER

Grave of Revolutionary War Vet. John Young (1760-1850) located in nearby Sand Run Cemetery. Noted soldier, Indian scout & trapper, he came to Kanawha Val., 1780s, named county trustee, 1794, and farmed 225 acres here.

After military service in Rev. War and Indian Wars, John Young and wife Keziah, Lewis Tackett's daughter, settled here (1801) on land granted by Va. Gov. Tyler. They raised 11 children on Young's Bottom farm, bordered by Sand Run Creek to Youngs Creek from Elk R. to Wills Creek. He helped build Fort Lee and defend Tackett's Fort, from which in 1790s raid he saved wife and infant son in daring escape in canoe.

US 119, at Sand Run Gospel Tabernacle, 4.3 miles north of Elkview bridge

PETROCHEMICAL PLANT

In 1920, Union Carbide built first plant for the production of synthetic organic chemicals from natural gas on a site directly across Elk River. From this nucleus grew the nation's giant petrochemical industry, employer of thousands.

US 119, near junction with WV 4, Clendenin

INDIAN MOUND

In 1883, the Smithsonian Institution excavated the South Charleston or Criel Mound. Thirteen skeletons were discovered, most of them in a large log tomb at base of the mound, along with a few grave offerings. The mound was built by the Adena Culture, about A.D. 1. It is the second largest in the State of West Virginia and the last of many mounds and earthworks that once were found in the Charleston area.

US 60 (MacCorkle Avenue), at junction with Oakes Street, South Charleston

ORDNANCE PLANT
This plant was built by the United States Government during the World War at a cost of over ten million dollars to supply armor plate for our navy. Nearby is one of the largest Indian mounds in the State.

US 60 West (MacCorkle Avenue), South Charleston

WASHINGTON'S LAND
The Mouth of Tyler Creek Tract of 2,950 acres was patented by George Washington on April 12, 1784, for services in French and Indian War. It bordered the Kanawha River "6 miles and 19 poles" and embraced the site of Dunbar.

*10th Street, near Dunbar Bridge, Dunbar

INDIAN MOUND/
MOUNDS EARTHWORKS
Here in the Shawnee Reservation is found an Indian mound which was probably excavated in 1884 by the Smithsonian Institution. The results of the archaeologists' work suggest that the mound was built between A.D. 1 and 500 by the Hopewellian

mound builders. At the base of the mound, the excavators found a crematory basin, and higher up in the mound, they found at least four skeletons.

One of the largest groups of mounds in the United States once existed in Dunbar, Institute, & South Charleston. In 1883-84, Smithsonian workers recorded 50 mounds and at least 10 earthworks (low earth embankments in geometric forms). Great Smith Mound, 35 ft. high and 175 in diameter, stood in Dunbar. The mounds in Shawnee Reservation & downtown South Charleston are all that remain today of these prehistoric works.

WV 25, Shawnee Park, Dunbar

WEST VIRGINIA STATE COLLEGE
Founded as West Virginia Colored Institute in 1891, renamed West Virginia Collegiate Institute in 1915 and West Virginia State College in 1929. Voluntarily desegregated in 1954. First state public four-year college and U.S. black land-grant college to be fully accredited.

WV 25, in front of Wallace Hall, Institute

MORGAN KITCHEN MUSEUM
Constructed in 1846. This cabin served as kitchen house for the 600-acre estate of John Morgan. The day before the Battle of Scary, on July 16, 1861, Union troops commanded by Gen. Jacob D. Cox camped on the Morgan estate and were fed from this kitchen. Donated to the city of St. Albans by Albert Sidney

Johnson Morgan, 1883-1973, this historic cabin was restored and is now known as Morgan Plantation Kitchen Museum.

US 60 West (MacCorkle Avenue), 1.8 miles east of Sattes Bridge, St. Albans

WASHINGTON'S LAND
George Washington's "Cole" River Tract of 2,000 acres was surveyed by John Floyd in 1774 and patented April 12, 1774. Bounded by the Coal and Kanawha Rivers, "5 miles and 88 poles", it embraced the site of St. Albans.

US 60 West (MacCorkle Avenue) in roadside park, 0.4 miles east of Sattes Bridge, St. Albans

FORT TACKETT
Nearby stood Fort Tackett, destroyed by Indians, 1790. Near the fort the day before the attack, Mrs. John Young gave birth to a son, the first white child born in this valley. The Youngs and a few others escaped to Fort Lee.

US 35, 0.2 miles north of junction with US 60, St. Albans

LEWIS COUNTY

Formed, 1816, from Harrison. Named for Colonel Charles Lewis who was killed at the Battle of Point Pleasant in 1774. Home of Jesse Hughes, frontier scout, and boyhood home of General Thomas J. "Stonewall" Jackson.

US 19/WV 4, Lewis-Braxton border; US 33, Lewis-Gilmer; US 19, Lewis-Harrison

Joseph A.J. Lightburn

*border; *US 33, Lewis-Upshur border; *WV 4, Lewis-Upshur border*

GENERAL LIGHTBURN
The Broad Run Baptist Church was organized in 1804. (2 Mi. W.) In its cemetery are buried many early settlers. Here is grave of Gen. Jos. A. Lightburn of the Union Army. After the War between the States, he became a Baptist minister.

US 19, at junction with Broad Run Road, Jane Lew

FIRST M.P. CHURCH
Two miles east stands the Old Harmony Church, which was built in 1819. In this church in 1829, John Mitchell and David Smith organized the first Methodist Protestant Church. Mitchell was its first pastor. Near the churchyard is his grave.

**US 19, Jane Lew*

HACKER'S CREEK/JANE LEW
At mouth of Jesse's Run was home of Jesse Hughes, Indian fighter and

scout. About 1770, John Hacker settled here. Near by is scene of Cozad and other border massacres. Several Indian villages and burying grounds were here.

Here Fort West was built, 1770-1773, by Edmund West and sons and burned by the Indians, 1778. Beech's Fort was later erected near by during the Indian wars. A mill was built here by Henry McWhorter in 1793.

US 19, at junction with Brook Run Road, Jane Lew

JACKSON'S MILL

Site of boyhood home of Gen. Thomas J. "Stonewall" Jackson. The first mill was built about 1808 by his grandfather, Col. Edward Jackson, who became a leader in border affairs. It is now the site of the W.Va. 4-H Camp for Boys and Girls.

County Route 1, at entrance to mill

JACKSON'S MILL/ JACKSON GRAVES

Boyhood home (2 Mi. W.) of Gen. Thomas J. "Stonewall" Jackson. First mill was built about 1808 by grandfather, Col. Edward Jackson, a leader in border affairs. Now site of the West Virginia 4-H Camp for Boys and Girls.

Two miles west in the old Jackson Cemetery are buried Colonel Edward Jackson and Elizabeth Jackson, the grandparents of General Stonewall Jackson with whom he lived until he became a Cadet at West Point Military Academy.

US 19, at entrance to Jackson's Mill Historic Area

JACKSON'S MILL

Boyhood home of General Thomas J. "Stonewall" Jackson. (4 Mi. W.) The first mill was built about 1808

Jackson's Mill, boyhood home of Confederate General "Stonewall" Jackson, circa 1900. The two-story house is shown in center, with the mill at right and the West Fork River circling around in the foreground.

by his grandfather, Colonel Edward Jackson, who became a leader in border affairs. It is now the site of the West Virginia 4-H Camp for Boys and Girls.

US 19, at junction with County Route 12 (Jackson's Mill Road)

GRAVES OF HEROES
In the Butcher Cemetery are the graves of many pioneer settlers, dating back more than 100 years. Here lies Paulser Butcher. Of seven Butcher brothers in the Revolution with Washington, four were killed in action.

*County Route 1, Turnertown

WESTON
Established, 1818, on farm of Henry Flesher, Revolutionary War veteran, first settler. He was attacked by Indians in 1784, but made his escape. Here is grave of Alexander Scott Withers, who told the story of "Border Warfare".

US 19 (Center Street), Weston

WESTON STATE HOSPITAL
Authorized as a western asylum by the state of Virginia in 1858. Construction was started in 1860, completed by the new State, and opened in 1864 as a hospital for the mentally ill. This is the largest hand-cut stone building in America.

US 33/US 119, hospital lot, Weston

WESTON STATE HOSPITAL
The oldest State institution in West Virginia was authorized by an act of General Assembly of Virginia, March 22, 1858. The War Between the States delayed the construction. It was not opened for patients until October 22, 1864.

US 33/US 119, Weston

LOUIS BENNETT LIBRARY
Home of Jonathan M. Bennett built 1875 and used as family home until 1922. Given by Mrs. Louis Bennett to county as public library to honor her husband and son. J.M. Bennett (1816-87) was active in state political and local business affairs in Virginia and West Virginia as was his son Louis (1848-1918). Grandson Louis (1894-1918) was killed while serving as World War I pilot.

US 19 (Court Street), Weston

WITHERS' GRAVE
In the old Arnold Cemetery on the hill are the graves of Alexander Scott Withers, born 10-12-1792, died 1-23-1865 and his wife, Malinda F., born 6-1-1793, died 9-15-1854. He was the author of "Chronicles of Border Warfare".

US 19, Weston

JOHN HACKER'S SETTLEMENT
John Hacker (1743-1824) erected his pioneer cabin about one mile west of here in 1769. He was the first white settler in Lewis County, and in the watershed of the creek which bears his name. He served under General George Rogers Clark in the Illinois campaign of 1778. Hacker

Johnson Newlon Camden

and his wife Mary are buried in a small private cemetery near here.

County Route 7, near Berlin

BENNETT-CAMDEN

Here was born Jonathan M. Bennett, (1816-1887). First auditor of Virginia and a leader in the two Virginias. Near here was born Johnson Newlon Camden (1828-1908), U.S. Senator, railroad builder and industrial leader.

*US 19, Walkersville

FORT PICKENS

Two miles east is the site of Fort Pickens where Capt. Morgan Darnall's Company A, 10th West Virginia Infantry, Vols., enrolled and built fort, 1861-62; mustered into Union Army by Capt. Bainbridge on March 13, 1862. Burned, 1864.

US 19, at junction with County Route 50 (Ireland Wildcat Road), near Ireland

FORT PICKENS/ ENGAGEMENTS OF CO. A

120 yds., northeast, Co. A 10th W.Va. Vol. Inf., built Fort Pickens for head-quarters and defense. Company raised by Capt. Morgan A. Darnall; mustered into U.S. service March 13, 1862. In several battles down to Appomattox.

Among the battles of Company A 10th W.Va. Vol. Inf. were Beverly, Droop Mt., Harpers Ferry, Opequon, Winchester, Leetown, Kernstown, Cedar Creek, Fishers Hill, Berryville, Petersburg Siege and the Appomattox surrender.

County Route 50 (Ireland Wildcat Road), approximately 3 miles east of US 19, Duffy

LINCOLN COUNTY

Formed in 1867 from Cabell, Kanawha, Boone and Putnam. Named for Abraham Lincoln, the sixteenth president of the United

J.H. Diss Debar sketch of President Abraham Lincoln, for whom Lincoln County is named

States. Producer of oil, gas and coal. Also noted for high quality of tobacco grown on its agricultural lands.

*WV 3, Lincoln-Boone border; *WV 10, Lincoln-Cabell border; *WV 214, Lincoln-Kanawha border; *WV 10, Lincoln-Logan border; WV 34, Lincoln-Putnam border; *WV 37, Lincoln-Wayne border

HAMLIN

Hamlin became county seat, 1869. First court met, 1867, at Hamline Church (1 Mi. away), where, 1852-53, the Virginia Legislature established town of Hamline, named for Bishop Leonidas Lent Hamline of the Methodist Episcopal Church.

*WV 3, roadside park, Hamlin

Test pilot Chuck Yeager, a native of Myra in Lincoln County, was the first man to fly faster than the speed of sound. Yeager is shown here at the 1987 ceremony to dedicate a statue in his honor in Hamlin, where he grew up.

LINCOLN COUNTY PRIMARY CARE CENTER, INC.

Founded 1975 in a renovated store by people of Lincoln County. First in nation to be federally designated as rural health clinic under PL 95-210. Hailed as model care provider, successfully building on community support, dedicated staff and Marshall Univ. School of Medicine. Honored in 1991 by National Rural Health Assoc. as nation's outstanding rural health practice.

WV 3, between Hamlin and West Hamlin

LOGAN COUNTY

Chief Logan

Formed in 1824 from Cabell, Kanawha, Giles and Tazewell. Named for Logan, the famous chief of the Mingo Indians, whose "Lament" is most noted example of Indian eloquence. Cornstalk's daughter, Aracoma, is buried in town of Logan.

*US 119, Logan-Boone border; *WV 10, Logan-Lincoln border; *WV 65, Logan-Mingo border; *WV 80, Logan-Mingo border; *US 119, Logan-Mingo border; WV 10, Logan-Wyoming border

HATFIELD CEMETERY

Capt. Anderson "Devil Anse" Hatfield, 1839-1921, is buried here. He was the leader of his clan in the bitter family feud with the McCoys.

A life-sized statue, modeled from photographs and imported from Italy, marks his grave.

WV 44, south of Stirrat

LOGAN

Here was home of Thomas Dunn English, mayor, 1852 to 1857, and author of "Ben Bolt". Aracoma, daughter of Cornstalk and the wife of Bolling Baker, the white renegade, was killed when settlers and Indians fought. She is buried here.

*US 119/WV 10, Logan

BATTLE OF BLAIR MT.

In August of 1921, 7000 striking miners led by Bill Blizzard met at Marmet for a march on Logan to organize the southern coalfields for the UMWA. Reaching Blair Mt. on August 31, they were repelled by deputies and mine guards, under Sheriff Don Chafin, waiting in fortified positions. The five-day battle ended with the arrival of U.S. Army and Air Corps. UMWA organizing efforts in southern WV were halted until 1933.

*WV 17, approximately 8 miles east of Logan between Ethel and Blair

Bill Blizzard

MARION COUNTY

Formed, 1842, from Harrison and Monongalia. Named for hero of the Revolution, Gen. Francis Marion. County was home of Francis H. Pierpont, leader in formation of this State. The Monongahela River forms just above Fairmont.

*US 19, Marion-Harrison border; US 19, Marion-Monongalia border; County Route 73, Marion-Monongalia border; Old County Route 73, Marion-Taylor border; *US 250, Marion-Taylor border; *WV 310, Marion-Taylor border; US 250, Marion-Wetzel border

BOOTHSVILLE

Named for Captain James Booth, pioneer soldier and settler. He was killed by Indians, 1778, and his companion, Nathaniel Cochran, wounded and captured. William Grundy, brother of the noted Felix Grundy, was also killed by Indians near by.

County Route 73/73 (Old County Route 73), at junction with County Route 73/7 (Boothsville Road), Boothsville

FAIRMONT

Home of Francis H. Pierpont, whose services in the organization of this State are commemorated by his statue in Statuary Hall, Washington. He was governor under the Re-

Aerial view of Fairmont, date unknown

stored Government of the State of Virginia, 1861-1868.

US 250 (Adams Street), at junction with County Route 64 (Jefferson Street), Fairmont

THE COLONEL GEORGE S. "SPANKY" ROBERTS, USAF MEMORIAL BRIDGE

Named in honor of local American hero, "Spanky" Roberts (1918-84), grad. of Dunbar H.S. & WV State College. 1st African-Am. aviation cadet, Tuskegee, 1941. Comm. 2nd Lt. & pilot in 1942; flew over 100 missions in Africa, Europe, & Mid-East, commanded 99th Fighter Sq., and 332nd Fighter Group in WWII. Decorated for meritorious service in WWII, Korea & 25 year career.

First Street and Fairmont Avenue; Adams Street and Cleveland Avenue, Fairmont

FAIRMONT STATE COLLEGE

Founded through private enterprise in 1865. Established as a state institution in 1867 and known as Fairmont State Normal School. Became Fairmont State Teachers College, 1931. Name Fairmont State College was adopted in 1943.

US 19, at junction with Locust Avenue, Fairmont

FIRST FATHER'S DAY SERVICE

Site of Williams Memorial Methodist Episcopal Church, now Central United Methodist, where Father's Day was first observed on July 5, 1908. Rev. Webb conducted service

84

upon request of Mrs. Charles Clayton, daughter of Meth. minister Fletcher Golden, just two months after first Mother's Day observance at Grafton. National recognition of Father's Day achieved in 1972 by congressional resolution.

US 250 (Fairmont Avenue), at junction with WV 310 (3rd Street), Fairmont

BOAZ FLEMING 1758-1830
Here in 1819, on land purchased of Thomas Barns, Boaz Fleming, pioneer, soldier of the American Revolution, founded his town, which, in 1820, the Virginia General Assembly established as Middletown, under a trustee form of government. Middletown was renamed Fairmont in 1843.

US 250 (Adams Street), courthouse square, Fairmont

CONFEDERATE CEMETERY
Near this point, in a mass grave, lie the remains of 39 Confederate soldiers from the 6th, 7th, 11th and 12th

Virginia cavalry unit—part of the force led by Gen. W. E. Jones. Attacked Fairmont April 29, 1863, after raids at Kingwood and Morgantown. The rebels routed the small Union forces, destroyed four railroad bridges, stole horses and cattle, and looted stores in town.

WV 310 (3rd Street), 0.4 miles south of US 250, Fairmont

PRICKETT'S FORT
To the north stood fort built, 1774, by Jacob Prickett. In 1777, Captain William Haymond commanded a militia company here, which guarded Monongahela Valley. In Prickett Cemetery are graves of Colonel Zackquill Morgan and other pioneers.

County Route 73, at junction with old County Route 73, northeast of Fairmont

FORT PAW PAW
North on high flat, overlooking the junction of Paw Paw Creek and the

This 1976 photo shows the reconstructed Prickett's Fort.

Monongahela River, was "Paw Paw Fort", a ninety-foot square stockade-fort erected in 1781. Rangers commanded by Captain Jack Evans garrisoned it.

US 19, near Rivesville-Fairview Road, Rivesville

DAVID MORGAN

Near this spot, 1779, David Morgan killed two Indians, of whose attack on his two children he had been warned in a strange dream. Morgan lived on a farm on the Monongahela River between Paw Paw and Prickett Creeks.

US 19, Rivesville

BARRACKVILLE COVERED BRIDGE

This covered bridge, built in 1853 by Eli and Lemuel Chenoweth, West Virginia's pioneer bridge builders, is an excellent example of a modified Burr Truss and is in substantially original condition. The bridge was saved from destruction during Jones' Raid, April 29, 1863, by the Ice family, nearby mill owners and Southern sympathizers. It's the only covered bridge in the state that bears its vehicular loads with essentially no modern reinforcement.

County Route 21, at junction with County Route 250/32, Barrackville

WAITMAN T. WILLEY

A mile north stood the cabin in which Waitman T. Willey, the State's first U.S. Senator, was born, October 18, 1811. Elected August 4, 1863 by the Legislature, he served until

Waitman T. Willey

March 3, 1871. Died May 2, 1900; buried in Morgantown.

WV 218, just north of US 250, Farmington

INDIAN MASSACRE

Here Nicholas Wood and Jacob Straight were killed and Mrs. Elizabeth Dragoo captured during Indian raid in 1786. Mrs. Straight and daughter made their escape from the Indians by hiding under sheltering rocks near by.

US 250, near Farmington

MANNINGTON/FLAGGY MEADOW

Once called Koontown but renamed in 1856 when chartered as town by Va. Assembly. Incorporated under W.Va. law in 1871. Abundant natural gas attracted diverse industry by 1900. Brick, glass and boiler factories, machine shops, granite works, Bowers Pottery Co., among world's largest sanitary products maker, & Phillips Tool Co., serving the coal, oil and gas industries, were located here.

One mi. south at Flaggy Meadow is site of the first oil well in the Mannington field, drilled 11 Oct. 1889. Location was scientifically verified by geologist I.C. White (1848-1927) using the anticlinal theory. Oil and gas boom sparked industrial growth in Mannington. Also at Flaggy Meadow is uncommon round barn built by Amos Hamilton in 1912 at cost of $1,900.

US 250, at junction with County Route 11 (Flaggy Meadow Road), just east of Mannington

COON'S FORT

To south, Indian fort built in 1777 under direction of Captain James Booth. It was an important place of refuge for many early settlers in this valley. Near by was the iron furnace built by Benjamin Brice in 1812.

US 19, 0.6 miles north of junction with WV 218, near Worthington

MONONGAH DISASTER

On the 6th of Dec., 1907 361 coal miners, many of them from countries far across the sea, perished under these hills in the worst mining disaster of our nation. The four who escaped died of injuries.

County Route 56, corner of Main Avenue and Bridge Street, Monongah

In December 1907, the worst mine disaster in U.S. history occurred at Monongah in Marion County.

MARSHALL COUNTY

Formed in 1835 from Ohio. Named for Chief Justice John Marshall. In Marshall County is Grave Creek Mound, first among remains left by the unknown race which lived in the Ohio Valley centuries before the white men came.

*WV 2, Marshall-Ohio border; WV 88, Marshall-Ohio border; *WV 89, Marshall-Wetzel border; WV 2, Marshall-Wetzel border; *US 250, Marshall-Wetzel border*

FORMAN MASSACRE

In the "Narrows", September 27, 1777, Captain Wm. Forman (Foreman) and his Hampshire County troops were ambushed by Indians. These men had joined the garrison of Fort Henry in protecting settlements on the Ohio against Indians.

WV 2/US 250, near McMechen

FORT WETZEL

John Wetzel and sons, Lewis, Jacob, Martin, John, and George, came with the Zanes in 1769 and built a fort. The Wetzels became famous as scouts and Indian fighters. In 1787, the elder Wetzel was killed by Indians at Baker's Station.

US 250, 0.3 miles from junction with WV 88, Limestone

FORT BEELER

Site of Indian fort built in 1779 on land of George Beeler. In 1782, an attack of Mohawk and Shawnee Indians was repulsed by its defenders, among whom were Martin and Lewis Wetzel, the celebrated scouts and Indian fighters.

US 250, Beeler's Station

MOUNDSVILLE/ CAPT. JAMES HARROD

Named for Grave Creek Mound. This mound, 900 feet around, 70 feet high, is the largest conical mound in America. The inscribed stone found in it has never been deciphered. Near by was the Indian fort built by Joseph Tomlinson.

Capt. James Harrod assembled 31 men at the mouth of Grave Creek in the spring of 1774 and from this point went to Kentucky. Their settlement at Harrodsburg was halted while they joined Capt. Christian's company in Dunmore's War.

7th Street, in front of Courthouse, Moundsville

GRAVE CREEK MOUND

This world-famous burial mound was built by the Adena people sometime before the Christian Era. The mound was originally 69 feet high, 295 feet in diameter, and was encircled by a moat. There were many mounds in the area—hence the city's name: Moundsville. In 1838, the Grave Creek Mound was tunnelled into and two log tombs with several burials and grave offerings were found.

Jefferson Avenue, at entrance to Grave Creek Mound, Moundsville

Grave Creek Mound is now the centerpiece of a historic park, including a 1930s-era museum which is now closed. A new museum was built in the 1970s.

WEST VIRGINIA PENITENTIARY
Established, 1866. A prison for men and women convicted of felonies until prison for women was established at Pence Springs, 1947. Capital criminals were hanged here, 1889-1950. Electric chair used until death penalty was abolished, 1965.

900 block of Jefferson Avenue, Moundsville

ROSBY'S ROCK
At Rosby's Rock (5 Mi. E.), Dec. 24, 1852, the B. & O. Railroad joined Baltimore and Wheeling with the first continuous railroad from the Atlantic to the Ohio, after such engineering feats as building 11 tunnels and 113 bridges.

WV 2, at junction with 12th Street, Moundsville

"BIG INCH" AND "LITTLE BIG INCH"
These War Emergency pipelines, 24" and 20" in diameter, which cross here, were constructed in 1943-44 during World War II. They transported crude oil and refined products from Texas to the oil starved Eastern Seaboard at a time when German U-boats were sinking tankers faster than they could be built. These lines are now owned and operated by Texas Eastern Transmission Corp. for transporting natural gas.

*WV 2, southwest of Moundsville

89

It took more than 24 years, but on Dec. 24, 1852, two Baltimore & Ohio (B&O) Railroad crews, one working west from Baltimore, the other pushing east from Wheeling, met at this point in the Grave Creek Valley about 18 miles southeast of Wheeling, completing the 370-mile-long railroad. At the time, it was the longest railroad in the world.

WASHINGTON'S LAND
This tract of 587 acres in Round Bottom was patented by George Washington in 1784 after a purchase of warrants held by officers of the French and Indian War. Washington sold these lands in 1798 to Archibald McClean.

WV 2, south of Moundsville

ZACHARY TAYLOR/ GEORGE ROGERS CLARK
General Zachary Taylor, on his way to Washington to be inaugurated as the 12th President of the U.S., found his steamer blocked by ice here. He left his boat and completed his trip over the National Pike.

In 1772, George Rogers Clark explored the Ohio and Great Kanawha rivers. He stayed the winter here, planted and harvested a crop, and carried out much surveying. Riflemen from the region aided him in winning the Northwest in 1778-1779.

WV 2, 0.4 miles south of junction with County Route 27 (Woodlands/Graysville Road)

BAKER'S STATION
Site of blockhouse built by Captain John Baker in 1784. Rendezvous of scouts along Indian warpath from Muskingum Valley into Virginia. Near by are buried Captain Baker, John Wetzel, and others killed by Indians in 1787.

WV 2, 0.4 miles south of junction with County Route 27 (Woodlands/Graysville Road)

MASON COUNTY
Formed, 1804, from Kanawha. Named for George Mason. Here Virginia frontiersmen, under Gen. Andrew Lewis, cleared way for American independence, 1774, by defeating federated western tribes under Chief Cornstalk.

*WV 2, Mason-Cabell border; WV 2, Mason-Jackson border; *US 33, Mason-Jackson border; *US 35, Mason-Putnam border; *WV 62, Mason-Putnam border

HARMONY BAPTIST CHURCH
The Reverend William George and sixteen charter members organized the Harmony Baptist Church in 1812. Congregation, affiliated with American Baptist churches, met in the Sullivan Meeting House from 1838-60. After 1842, meetings alternated with Harmony Meeting House. Present sanctuary was the original church built and dedicated in 1860.

*US 35, 15 miles southeast of Point Pleasant

GENERAL MCCAUSLAND
Home of General John McCausland, 1836-1927, one of the last officers of the general staff of the Confederate Army. He served in Pennsylvania, the Virginias, and Maryland. He led Lomax's cavalry against Sheridan in Valley Campaign.

US 35, 0.4 miles west of Putnam County line

"LOST COLONY"

In 1772, Washington patented 10,990 acres along the Great Kanawha River. In 1775, he had James Cleveland and William Stevens lead colonist there. Land was cleared; orchards planted; houses built. But when war ended, colony was gone.

US 35, 8.5 miles east of junction with WV 2, Southside

VIRGIL A. LEWIS

Educator and historian born near West Columbia, July 6, 1848; died in Mason City, December 5, 1912; was buried in Point Pleasant. He founded the Southern Historical Magazine in 1892; was State Superintendent of Schools, 1893-97; first State Historian and Archivist, 1905-12; author of many books. How West Virginia Was Made, History and Government of West Virginia, and Hand Book of West Virginia are among the best known.

US 33, at junction with Brown Street, 0.6 miles north of WV 62, Mason

"MARK TWAIN" FAMILY

Samuel and Pamela Clemens, grandparents of "Mark Twain", settled here in 1803. Samuel was accidently killed in 1805 at a "house-raising". Their eldest son, John Marshall, the father of "Mark Twain", lived here until he moved West.

*WV 62, about 3 miles north of Leon

LAKIN STATE HOSPITAL

Established in 1919 by an act of the Legislature. Opened for colored patients in 1926 and integrated in 1954. In 1957, the Hospital acquired the former Boys Industrial School. A rehabilitation center has since been added to the Hospital.

WV 62, Lakin

The former Lakin State Hospital is now operated as a long-term care facility by the West Virginia Department of Health and Human Resources. Date unknown.

DR. JESSE BENNETT

Grave and home (1/2 mile W.) of Dr. Jesse Bennett, whose Ceasarean operation on his wife, 1794, was the first in America. Bennett, colonel of Virginia Militia, 1804-1814, refused to aid Blennerhassett, Burr in their ambitious plan.

WV 62, at junction with 9th Street, Point Pleasant

FORT ROBINSON

Near here stood the blockhouse built by Captain Isaac Robinson in 1794. Indians attacked the fort soon after its erection but the little garrison drove them away. Robinson had spent 12 years as an Indian captive and was a noted border scout.

*WV 62, north of Point Pleasant

POINT PLEASANT/ POINT PLEASANT

About 1771 was proposed as the capital of a new colony, "Vandalia." It was visited by early explorers: La Salle, 1669; Celeron, 1749; Gist, 1750; and Washington, 1770. Daniel Boone had a trading post here.

Fort Blair, was built here in 1774 and later Fort Randolph, the center of Indian activities, 1777-1778. Here are graves of "Mad Anne" Bailey, border scout, and Cornstalk, Shawnee chief, held hostage and killed here in 1777.

WV 2, at junction with 6th Street, courthouse square, Point Pleasant

"Battle of Point Pleasant"
Miniature of a painting done by Joseph Faris of Wheeling, 1902

POINT PLEASANT BATTLE/ WAR OF 1812

Here, Oct. 10, 1774, General Andrew Lewis and a thousand Virginia riflemen defeated the federated Indian tribes led by Cornstalk. Known as the "first battle of the Revolution." It was the most important battle between Indians and whites.

On October 20, 1812, the western Virginia Brigade of Militia under command of General Joel Leftwich, embarked here for the Ohio frontier to join the Northwestern Army for service in the Second War with England.

Main Street, at junction with 1st Street, Battle Monument Park, Point Pleasant

ANDREW & CHARLES LEWIS MARCH

The nearby highway is part of route traversing W.Va. from Lewisburg to Point Pleasant memorialized by the state to commemorate the march of the American Colonial army of 1,200 men led by Andrew & Charles Lewis. After a month's march this army defeated a Shawnee Indian force led by Cornstalk at the Battle of Point Pleasant on the banks of the Ohio & Kanawha rivers, October 10, 1774.

WV 2, east entrance of Krodel Park, Point Pleasant

BOONE'S TRADING POST

Daniel Boone, noted scout and Indian fighter, operated trading post here, 1790. He was scout for General Lewis enroute to Point Pleasant, 1774. Named County Lieuten-

ant for Kanawha and served this county in the Virginia Assembly.

WV 2, west entrance of Krodel Park, Point Pleasant

"BORDER GRAYS"

Organized at Barboursville, Sept. 18, 1862, with Captain William Gunn as commander. Served with the Guyandotte Battalion until Jan. 1863, then was assigned as Company D, 8th Virginia Cavalry, CSA, under Col. Albert G. Jenkins.

4th Street, off WV 2, Point Pleasant

GEORGE ROGERS CLARK

From the Kanawha's mouth in May, 1778, George Rogers Clark set out to attack the British at Vincennes and Kaskaskia. The conquest of the Northwest by his little army of 175 men is ranked among the greatest exploits of all history.

WV 2, at junction with 6th Street, courthouse square, Point Pleasant

EARLY GRAVES

In Point Pleasant Cemetery are graves of John Roush and John Roseberry, Revolutionary War soldiers, Maj. Andrew Waggener, hero of Craney Island in the War of 1812, and others who were prominent in early history.

WV 62, at junction with 9th Street, Point Pleasant

GEN. JOHN MCCAUSLAND

On pinnacle (300 feet E.) overlooking his boyhood home is the grave of Gen. John McCausland, 1836-1927. He was conspicuous for his operations in the Shenandoah Valley, and for his raids into Maryland and Pennsylvania. He fought at Petersburg and Five Forks and on the retreat to Appomattox, cut his way through Federal lines before the surrender. Paroled at Charleston, West Virginia at close of the War.

WV 2, Henderson

MAY MOORE MOUND

This is one of the larger burial mounds in the State. It has never been properly excavated, but was probably built by the Adena people between 500 B.C. and A.D. 1. Several smaller mounds can also be seen in this area.

WV 2, 3 miles south of Gallipolis Ferry

MERCER'S BOTTOM/ CAPTAIN JOHN HEREFORD

This is part of the 16,000 acre tract surveyed by order of Washington for General Hugh Mercer. Nearby are the graves of Adjutant John Hereford and Ensign John Wilson. They were officers in the Revolutionary Army.

Revolutionary War Adjutant in Col. John Alexander's Virginia Regiment under Lafayette at Yorktown. He was born in Fairfax Co. in 1758, moved to Mason Co. in 1808, serving as magistrate and sheriff, and died, 1846.

WV 2, 1.5 miles north of Ashton

THOMAS HANNAN

Born 1755, died 1835. Soldier in the Revolution and the first white settler in Cabell County. Blazed trace

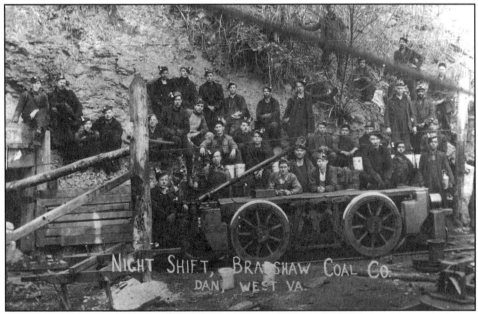

McDowell County coal miners in the early 1900s

The McDowell County Courthouse was the site of the 1921 murder of Matewan police chief Sid Hatfield. The death of Hatfield, who had defended the rights of striking miners, sparked an armed march on southern West Virginia.

from Saint Albans to Chillicothe which bears his name. This was the first road that came into Cabell and Mason counties. Hannan owned 5800 acres of land in these counties. He is buried in private cemetery nearby.

WV 2, near Mason-Cabell border

MCDOWELL COUNTY

Formed from Tazewell, 1858. Named for James McDowell, governor of Virginia from 1843 to 1846. County is famous for the production of bituminous coal. This county originally had four acres of coal for every acre of its land surface.

*US 52, McDowell-Mercer border; *US 52/WV 80, McDowell-Wyoming border; *WV 16, McDowell-Wyoming border*

WELCH

Incorporated, 1893, and named for Captain I.A. Welch, who led in the coal development of this county and founded the city. Here is the first memorial building erected in the United States to the memory of the veterans of World War I.

WV 16 (Wyoming Street), at junction with Bank Street, courthouse square, Welch; US 52, 1.1 miles from junction with WV 103, Welch

WELCH EMERGENCY HOSPITAL

This is a State institution. It was founded in 1900 and has been maintained as a general hospital for treatment of charity and semi-charity medical and surgical cases.

WV 16, at junction with County Route 7, Welch

The Welch Emergency Hospital, or "Miners' Hospital," date unknown

BARTLEY MINE DISASTER

Near here, in Bartley No. 1 shaft mine, on Jan. 10, 1940, fire and explosion killed ninety-one miners. The names of the men who lost their lives are inscribed on monument erected in the park by the United Mine Workers of America.

WV 83, near County Route 83/1 (Bartley Hollow Road), west of Bartley

LEWIS' CAMP

Here Major (later General) Andrew Lewis camped, February 26, 1756, with Virginia troops on way to attack Indians who had been raiding the settlements. Bitter cold and food shortage brought disaster to the expedition.

US 52, at junction with WV 80, Iaeger

MERCER COUNTY

Formed, 1837, from Giles and Tazewell. Named for General Hugh Mercer, Revolutionary War officer, who was mortally wounded at Princeton, 1777. This county, gateway to the South, is rich in fine farms and mineral deposits.

*US 52, Mercer-McDowell border; *US 19, Mercer-Raleigh border; WV 20, Mercer-Summers border; *WV 10, Mercer-Wyoming border; *US 19, Mercer-Virginia state border; *US 52, Mercer-Virginia state border

CAMP JONES

Here in 1862 was stationed the 23rd Ohio Regt., U.S.A. Encamped were Gen. J.D. Cox, Maj. R.B. Hayes and Sergt. William McKinley. All became governors of Ohio; Hayes and

McKinley became Presidents of the United States.

US 19, at junction with County Route 19/ 46, 0.6 miles south of Flat Top

RAVENCLIFF SAND

This pebbly massive Princeton Sandstone at the top of the Bluestone River Gorge is the "Ravencliff Sand" of the driller. It produces oil and natural gas in southern West Virginia.

I-77 northbound (West Virginia Turnpike), at Bluestone rest stop overlook

CONCORD COLLEGE

Chartered as Concord State Normal School, February 28, 1872. Classes began in 1875. Moved to present campus in 1910. Name was changed

to Concord State Teachers College in 1931 and to Concord College in 1943.

0.4 miles east of WV 20, Athens

WILLIAM FRENCH HOME

One mile east is the former home of Colonel William Henderson French, (1812-1872), local legislator, land dealer and soldier. Elected to the Virginia House of Delegates in 1842, 1843 and 1845, French later became a Captain in the Confederate cavalry in 1861 and was promoted to colonel in 1863. He was a large land holder in the region and once owned the entire site of the town of Athens.

WV 20, near secondary road 44/9, south of Athens

Colonel William Henderson French House near Athens

MITCHELL CLAY

Here Mitchell Clay settled in 1775. Eight years later Indians killed two of his children and captured his son, Ezekiel. Pursuers killed several of the Indians but the boy was taken into Ohio and burned at the stake.

US 19/WV 10, north of Kegley

RICHARD BLANKENSHIP

Richard Blankenship, Revolutionary War Soldier, was a member of Major James Robertson's company of New River Valley volunteers who fought at the Battle of Point Pleasant, October 10, 1774. He lived on a 33 acre farm 8 mi. southeast, at Ingleside, Mercer Co. and was recorded as an octogenarian in 1840 census. He was early settler, soldier and progenitor of many people in this area.

US 19/WV 20 (Main Street), at junction with Alvis Street, courthouse square, Princeton

PRINCETON

Scene of several actions, May, 1862, between Federal troops from General Cox's army and Confederate forces under Jenifer and Wharton. When the Confederates abandoned their camp here, the town was set on fire and partially burned.

US 19/WV 20 (Main Street), at junction with Scott Street, courthouse square, Princeton

BATTLE OF PIGEON'S ROOST

Near a hill south of town on May 1 Maj. Peter Otey surprised and routed a Union regiment commanded by Colonel Louis von Blessing. Federal losses were 18 killed, 56 wounded and 14 captured. Confederate losses were 1 killed, 9 wounded and none captured. Confederate dead from this skirmish and other clashes in the Princeton area are buried in Oakwood Cemetery.

US 19, 0.1 miles north of junction with WV 4, Princeton

BIG LIME

The Greenbrier Limestone, which crops out between here and Bluefield, is the "Big Lime" of the driller. Fish-egg like (oölitic) zones in the "Big Lime" yield oil and natural gas in West Virginia.

*US 19/US 460, Bluefield

BLUEFIELD

Bluefield is on land which John Davidson patented in 1774. With Richard Bailey he built a fort about 1777. Later he was killed by the Indians. The home, built by Joseph Davidson in 1811, is still standing.

US 52 (Bland Street), at junction with Federal Street, Bluefield

BLUEFIELD STATE TEACHERS COLLEGE

Established as the Bluefield Colored Institute by act of the Legislature in 1895. Later the school became an institution of higher learning for Negroes. Renamed and given its present title in 1929.

US 52, Conley Hall, Bluefield

BLUEFIELD STATE COLLEGE
Estab., 1895, by WV Leg. as Bluefield Colored Institute; 1929 became Bluefield State Teachers College. Renamed in 1943, Bluefield State College has continued providing quality higher education for all citizens of the area.

US 52, Conley Hall, Bluefield

ANDREW DAVIDSON
Site of the pioneer cabin of Andrew Davidson. While he was absent, Indians burned his cabin, tomahawked his children, and captured his wife. Mrs. Davidson was sold to a Canadian family from whom she was ransomed.

US 52 (Cumberland Road), Bluefield

PINNACLE ROCK
Erosion—Nature's cutting tool—has chiseled away the stone on this spur of Flat Top Mountain, leaving this giant cockscomb more than

2700 feet above sea level. Several counties may be seen from these cliffs.

US 52, Pinnacle Rock State Park

UPPER MAXON SAND
The resistant Stony Gap Sandstone forming Pinnacle Rock is the "Upper Maxon" of the driller. It produces oil and natural gas in southern West Virginia.

US 52, Pinnacle Rock State Park

BRAMWELL/
MILL CREEK COAL & COKE CO.
Called "Home of the Millionaires" when town's fourteen represented the greatest per capita concentration in the U.S. Incorporated in 1889, Bramwell was the business and residential community for Pocahontas coalfield owners and operators such as J.H. Bramwell, I.T. Mann, Edward Cooper, Philip Goodwill, John Hewitt and William Thomas until Depression ruined economy. Recognized by National Register of Historic Places, 1984.

John Cooper's mine in Cooper section of Bramwell shipped 1st coal from W. Virginia's valuable Pocahontas Coalfield over N&WRR on 4 Nov. 1884. The Coaldale, Caswell Creek & Booth-Bowen mines, operated by Cooper, Jones, Freeman, Booth & Bowen, were pioneer mines in the field. The Philadelphia financed Flat Top Coal Land Assoc., later Pocahontas Coal & Coke, became the coalfield's largest landholder.

County Route 120, at junction with County Route 20/9, Bramwell

JORDAN NELSON'S COAL BANK
Jordan Nelson, blacksmith, dug coal from bank to fuel forge, and made 1st commercial use by selling for 1 cent a bushel in 1870s. In 1873 I.A. Welch surveyed Pocahontas Coalfield for J. Hotchkiss who induced F.J. Kimball, later Pres. of N&WRR, to visit site May 1881. Southwest Va. Improvement Co. bought land and opened Pocahontas Mine and shipped coal over N&W's New River Line built to open coalfield.

County Route 120, west of Bramwell, 0.1 miles east of Virginia border

MINERAL COUNTY
Formed from Hampshire in 1866 and named for its great mineral deposits. In Mineral County is Fort Ashby, the only standing unit in the chain of frontier forts which were built in 1755 under George Washington's order.

*WV 93, Mineral-Grant border; *US 50/ WV 42, Mineral-Grant border; *US 50/ US 220, Mineral-Hampshire border; WV 28, Mineral-Hampshire border; *WV 46, Mineral-Maryland border; *WV 42, Mineral-Maryland border

FORT OHIO
To the north, Fort Ohio was built about 1750 by the Ohio Company as a storehouse and fortified in 1751. This post was abandoned later and a stronger fort, known as Fort Cumberland, erected at Wills Creek across the river.

*WV 28, Ridgeley

FORT SELLERS
On land Washington surveyed for Elias Sellers in 1748 stood this fort, important link in system of frontier defenses. It was garrisoned by an officer and thirty men and withstood several attacks by the Indians.

WV 28, south of Ridgeley

FORT ASHBY
Erected in 1755 by Lieut. John Bacon under orders from George Washington and garrisoned with twenty-one men. Lieut. Robert Rutherford, with company of Rangers, was defeated here, August, 1756, by the French and Indians. Fort was named for Col. John Ashby who arrived there after remarkable escape from the Indians. Ashby commanded the fort until after the Revolutionary War. The W.P.A. restored fort in 1939.

WV 28 and WV 46, Fort Ashby

FORT ASHBY
Fort Ashby, only standing unit in chain of Indian forts that Col. George Washington built along Virginia frontier, 1755. Sharp fighting here, 1756. In 1794, troops under Gen. Daniel Morgan camped here on way to suppress Whiskey Rebellion.

WV 28 and WV 46, in front of fort, Fort Ashby

ORISKANY-HELDERBERG

The massive sandstone at the top of the exposure is the Oriskany and the limestone in the quarry is the Helderberg of the driller and the geologist. The "Oriskany Sand", an important gas Sand, has produced in excess of a trillion cubic feet of gas in West Virginia.

*WV 46, 2 miles east of Keyser; *US 50, south of New Creek*

WASHINGTON'S HOST

At Reese's Mill, ruins of the home of Abraham Johnson, who entertained George Washington and surveying party in 1748. Johnson appeared in Patterson Creek Valley in 1735 and 1740 and in 1750 became an official of the Ohio Company.

WV 46, 1.5 miles east of County Route 9, east of Keyser

AVERELL'S RAID/KEYSER

Here in 1863 General W.W. Averell started the Federal Cavalry raid to Salem, Virginia, and then back into this State. This is among the great exploits of the War. Many of his troopers were from West Virginia.

Between 1861-1865, Keyser, then New Creek, was sought by the North and South. It changed hands fourteen times. Fort Fuller, where Potomac State College stands, was supported by a series of forts girding the town.

US 220 (South Mineral Street) and Carskadon Road, Keyser

POTOMAC STATE COLLEGE

Chartered, Feb. 15, 1901, as Keyser Preparatory Branch of West Virginia University. Became Potomac State School, 1921; Potomac State School of West Virginia University, 1935; Potomac State (junior) College, West Virginia University, 1953.

US 220 (Mineral Street), at junction with State Street, Keyser

MAYO AND SAVAGE

Near here, William Mayo, Thomas Savage, and party spent the winter of 1736 on their expedition for the British King to determine the headwaters of the Potomac River and fix the boundary between Maryland and the lands of Lord Fairfax.

WV 46, Piedmont

DR. JOHN GREEN

One-fourth mile south is grave of Dr. John Green, first resident doctor in Mineral County, 1832-73. Born in Bolton, Eng., November 13, 1798; came to Virginia in May, 1827, after serving as medic in Battle of Waterloo. Died Dec. 21, 1873.

WV 42 and County Route 4, about 2 miles south of Elk Garden

CLAYSVILLE UNITED METHODIST CHURCH

Congregation was organized in 1849. The church, constructed in 1850 of lumber produced on a water-powered sawmill and furnished with seats of chestnut, hand finished, is in an excellent state of preservation. It was first used as a com-

A riding party poses in front of the Vandiver-Trout-Clause House, circa 1900

bined church, school and community building. During the Civil War both Union and Confederate troops held services here, the time depending on who temporarily controlled the valley.

US 50, at junction with WV 93

VANDIVER-TROUT-CLAUSE HOUSE
Located on a 1766 Fairfax grant and site of a former blockhouse. Built by John Vandiver in early 19th century; soon operated as an ordinary. Henry Trout purchased the house in 1869, repairing damage done during the Civil War. In the latter half of the century the house was also a post office and polling place. In 1904 the property was sold to Henry Clause, the inn's last proprietor.

US 50/US 220, and County Route 9, near Ridgeville

DEVONIAN SHALE
The carbonaceous shale exposed in the picnic area is the Marcellus brown and black shale of the driller. It yields large amounts of natural gas in southern West Virginia.

*US 50, near Mineral-Hampshire border

MINGO COUNTY

The youngest county in the State was formed from Logan in 1895. It was named for the Mingo Indians, terror of the Virginia borders, whose chief was Logan. Robert Morris, financier of the Revolutionary Army, patented land here.

*WV 65, Mingo-Logan border; *WV 80, Mingo-Logan border; *US 119, Mingo-Logan border; *US 52, Mingo-Wayne border; *US 52, Mingo-Wyoming border; WV 49, Mingo-Kentucky border

THOMAS SMITH

Formerly a surveyor in Washington Co., Va., Smith was early settler on Horsepen Creek at mouth of Gilbert Creek. He served Revolutionary cause as a private in the Virginia militia unit organized for the 1776 punitive Cherokee Expedition under Col. William Christian's command. He was half brother to Valentine and Joe Hatfield, and progenitor of many southern West Va. families.

US 52, near junction with County Route 13, west of Gilbert

HORSEPEN MOUNTAIN

Nearby Bolling Baker, white leader of Shawnee Indians, and husband of Aracoma, the daughter of Chief Cornstalk, held horses stolen from the white settlements. Recovery by owners in effect exterminated Baker's adopted tribe.

US 52, near junction with WV 44, Mountain View

The Mingo Oak

THE MINGO OAK

The largest white oak in the United States when it died and was cut down, 9-23-1938. Age was estimated to be 582 years. Height, 146 feet; circumference, 30 feet, 9 inches; diameter, 9 feet, 9 1/2 inches. Trunk contained 15,000 feet B.M. lumber.

*County Route 65/5, near Ragland

HATFIELD-MCCOY FEUD

The death in 1882 of Ellison Hatfield, brother of "Devil Anse", from wounds he received in an election-day fight in Pike County, Kentucky, with three sons of Randolph McCoy, and their subsequent killing by the Hatfields, triggered America's most famous family feud. The feud continued six years across the Tug River and brought death to an untold number of Hatfields, McCoys, and their kinsmen.

WV 49 (Railroad Avenue), at junction with Laurel Street, Matewan

MATEWAN MASSACRE

In 1920 area miners went on strike to gain recognition of UMWA. On May 19 of the same year, twelve Baldwin-Felts Agency guards came from Bluefield to evict the miners from company houses. As guards left town, they argued with town police chief Sid Hatfield and Mayor Testerman. Shooting of undetermined origins resulted in the deaths of two coal miners, seven agents, and the mayor. None of the 19 men indicted were convicted.

Off Main Street, Matewan

Clan leader Anderson "Devil Anse" Hatfield, seated second from left, is shown with members of his extended family in 1897, several years after the end of the famous feud.

THE OHIO EXTENSION

Near this spot, the two sections of the greatest construction project undertaken by the Norfolk & Western RR were joined on Sept. 22, 1892. Starting from Kenova and Elkhorn two years earlier, its completion took 5,000 men and changed the line's character from that of a southern agrarian road into a major Atlantic-Midwest trunk route and mighty "Pocahontas Coal Carrier." Known since 1982 as Norfolk Southern. Dedicated by N&W Historical Society, June 19, 1992.

WV 49, about 4 miles south of Williamson

WILLIAMSON

Named for W.J. Williamson. Its site was a corn field in 1890. Now it is business center of vast coal fields. Early colonization efforts here were supported by John Peter Dumas, a relative of Alexandre Dumas, novelist.

*US 119/US 52, Williamson

Williamson, date unknown

LEWIS' EXPEDITION

Camp of Major (later General) Andrew Lewis in 1756, with Virginia troops, led by Smith, Hogg, Preston, Pearis, Woodson, and others, on way to attack Indians in Ohio. The Tug River and other streams were named by expedition.

US 52, East Kermit

MONONGALIA COUNTY

Formed, 1776, from District of West Augusta. All or parts of 21 other counties, including three in Pennsylvania, were carved from it. Named for the Monongahela River, bearing an Indian name, which means the "River of Caving Banks".

*US 19, Monongalia-Marion border; County Route 73, Monongalia-Marion border; *WV 7, Monongalia-Preston border; County Route 73, Monongalia-Preston border; US 119, Monongalia-Taylor border; *WV 7, Monongalia-Wetzel border*

SALT SAND

The massive pebbly Connoquenessing Sandstone, one of the "Salt Sands" of the driller, forms Coopers Rock. The "Salt Sands" produce oil and natural gas in West Virginia and commercial brines on the Kanawha and Ohio Rivers.

County Route 73, Coopers Rock State Forest

HENRY CLAY FURNACE

West, in Coopers Rock State Forest, is the Henry Clay cold blast furnace, built 1834-36 by Leonard Lamb. It had capacity of four tons of pig iron per day, and furnished employment for 200 people. Sold to Ellicots in 1837. Operated until 1847.

County Route 73, Coopers Rock State Forest

ICE'S FERRY

Ice's Ferry was settled by Frederick Ice in 1767. His son, Adam, born the same year, was the first white child born in Monongahela Valley. Andrew Ice in 1785 started the first authorized ferry in western Virginia.

County Route 73, at Cheat Lake

STEWARTSTOWN

William Stewart settled here in 1771. Northeast was Fort Dinwiddie. Pioneer minister John Corbley, whose wife and three children were killed in 1782 Indian raid on Garard's Fort, founded Forks of Cheat Baptist Church here in 1775.

US 119, at junction with County Route 65 (Stewartstown Road), Stewartstown

FORT MARTIN

Fort Martin was built in 1769 by Colonel Charles Martin. Three settlers were killed and seven captured by Indians near the fort in 1779. At the Methodist Episcopal Church here Bishop Francis Asbury preached in 1784.

County Route 53 (Fort Martin Road), 4 miles north of junction with WV 100, Fort Martin

END OF MASON-DIXON SURVEY

Directional Marker: Approach to the High Ridge where this Survey ended, Oct. 18, 1767. The present Pennsylvania-West Virginia Line Stone Marker is dated 1883. The Line was extended to the Southwest corner of Pennsylvania in 1784.

WV 39, foot of Brown's Hill

CATAWBA WAR PATH

Branch of Warrior Trail of the Great Catawba Indian War Path located here where Mason and Dixon Survey crossed Dunkard Creek for third time. Guide, Six Nations Indians' chief, declared he "would not proceed one step further," because hostile Delaware and Shawnee Indians had ordered them to halt. On Oct. 18, 1767, western end of original Mason-Dixon Line was set on the next high peak, Brown's Hill.

County Route 39, at Mason-Dixon Historical Park; County Route 39, east of Mason-Dixon Historical Park

BORDER HEROINE

During the Indian raids in 1779 upon the settlements on Dunkard Creek, savages attacked the cabin of John Bozarth. Armed only with an axe, in a brief hand-to-hand fight, Mrs. Bozarth killed three of the men.

WV 7, at junction with County Route 39, near Core

STATLER'S FORT

John Statler built a fort here in 1770. In its vicinity a number of settlers were Indian victims in 1777 and 18 white men lost their lives the next year. Later Statler himself and companions were massacred.

WV 7, near Blacksville

Main Street, Blacksville, date unknown

BLACKSVILLE

Site of Baldwin blockhouse, 1770-1775. Brice and Nathan Worley settled here in 1766. Nathan was killed by Indians in 1777. Laid out as a town in 1829 and lots sold through a lottery. Town is named for David Black, early settler.

WV 7, near junction with WV 218, Blacksville

MASON-DIXON LINE

Made famous as line between free and slave states before War Between the States. The survey establishing Maryland-Pennsylvania boundary began, 1763; halted by Indian wars, 1767; continued to southwest corner, 1782; marked, 1784.

*WV 218, 0.1 miles from junction with WV 7, at West Virginia-Pennsylvania border; *US 119, Monongalia-Pennsylvania border; *US 19, Monongalia-Pennsylvania border*

FORT PIERPONT

John Pierpont, Revolutionary soldier and the son-in-law of Zackquill Morgan, built a fort in 1769. Washington was his guest in 1784. Here was born Francis H. Pierpont, who played an important part in the formation of West Virginia.

County Route 67, at junction with North Pierpont Road and County Route 73/12, north of Morgantown

EASTON ROLLER MILL

Steam driven grist mill, built ca. 1870 by Henry Koontz, could grind 120 bu. of grain daily. Stone burrs were replaced with iron rollers in 1894, improving output and quality, and representing peak technological development for a local flour mill. Several owners operated mill before changes in marketing and consumer habits, coupled with reduced local grain supply, forced closing in 1930.

US 119, at junction with County Route 119/17, north of Morgantown

201ST INFANTRY/ FIELD ARTILLERY

This National Guard unit traces its origins to Capt. Morgan Morgan, who formed the company Feb. 17, 1735. It served with Washington's militia in Braddock's 1755 campaign. At the outset of the Revolution he called upon these fighting men to "drive the invaders from our land." One of the oldest and still active military units, the 201st has fought or trained men for every conflict involving the U.S.

Willowdale Road, near junction with Chestnutridge Road (WV 705), Morgantown

WILLEY-WADE-WHITE/ MORGANTOWN

A trio of Monongalia County men have made large gifts to the world. Waitman T. Willey led in setting up this State. Alexander L. Wade first demonstrated a system of graded schools. Dr. I.C. White was a leader in field of geology.

Settlement of Thomas Decker, 1758, destroyed by Indians. Settled, 1766-

Israel Charles White was the first state geologist.

68, by Colonel Zackquill Morgan. Colonel John Evans came in 1769. Incorporated as town, 1785. State College of Agriculture established in 1867 and made into State University in 1868.

WV 7, Courthouse Square, Morgantown

FIRST POTTERY/OLD IRON WORKS

The first pottery in West Virginia was founded here about 1785 and the making of pottery was important before 1800. John Scott, Jacob Foulk, John Thompson, and Francis Billingsley were among the first potters.

Iron furnaces were busy in Monongalia County at early date. At Rock Forge, Samuel Hanway started work, 1798, and on Cheat River, Samuel Jackson built a furnace. The latter plant, under the Ellicotts, worked 1200 men.

Walnut Street, near junction with US 119, Morgantown

OLD STONE HOUSE

Oldest stone house in Monongalia County. By legend built by Jacob

Nuze on original lot 25. Sold 1795 to tavern-keeper Henry Dering. Owned 1800-1813 by potters John Thompson and Jacob Foulk. Bought by Joseph Shackelford who operated a tanyard here for 50 years. A minister, he led the first Methodist reform movement in area. First Methodist-Protestant Church formed here, 1830. Sold to Frank Cox and George Baker, 1895. Used as dwelling and tailor shop. Occupied by Morgantown Service League, 1935, and restored to near original condition for use as headquarters and shop. House donated to League by Cox heirs, 1976.

Chestnut Street, between house and city parking garage, Morgantown

WEST VIRGINIA UNIVERSITY

Founded by the Legislature on February 7, 1867, as the Agricultural College of West Virginia under terms of the Federal Land-Grant Act of 1862. On December 4, 1868, the name was changed to West Virginia University.

*US 19/WV 7, at entrance to parking lot of Core Arboretum, northwest of Morgantown; *US 19, Westover; *US 119, Dorsey's Knob*

DUNKARD SANDS

The Buffalo and Mahoning sandstones, the "Dunkard Sands" of the driller, are exposed in the road cuts and merge to form a great cliff at Raven Rock. They produce oil and natural gas in northern and western West Virginia.

County Route 73, 1.5 miles south of junction with US 119, Uffington

HARMONY GROVE CHURCH
Built before the Civil War on land donated by Rufus E. and Elizabeth Conn in 1854, this church was the meetinghouse for congregations of Episcopal, Presbyterian, Methodist Episcopal and Methodist Protestant denominations. It was placed on the National Register in 1983.

County Route 45, 2.5 miles from junction with US 19, Harmony Grove

DENTS RUN COVERED BRIDGE
1.5 miles south; erected in 1889 by order of Monongalia County Court. Contract awarded to W.A. Loar with Edward W. Brand as superintendent. Stone abutments built by Loar at cost of $198, with wood framework constructed by Wm. and Joseph Mercer at a cost of $250. Bridge is 40 ft. long, 13 ft. wide, and uti-

lizes the Kingpost truss design. Last covered bridge still standing in county.

US 19, at junction with County Route 43, near Laurel Point

JONES' RAID
Over this route through the Monongahela Valley, April 27-29, 1863, General William E. Jones led his division of General John D. Imboden's Confederate army. This raid concluded with the destruction of the oil fields on the Little Kanawha River.

US 19, south of Morgantown near the Marion County line

MONROE COUNTY
Formed in 1799 from Greenbrier. Named for President James Monroe. In this county lived Col. Andrew S. Rowan who, 1898, carried

Built in 1833, Old Sweet Springs (Andrew Rowan Memorial Home) is considered to be one of America's oldest mineral water resorts. The resort was purchased by the state in 1941 and served as a home for the elderly until the 1990s.

the news of American intervention to General Y Iniguez Garcia, leader of the Cubans.

WV 3, Monroe-Greenbrier border; US 219, Monroe-Greenbrier border; WV 12, Monroe-Summers border

ROWAN MEMORIAL HOME
Established as a home for the aged by act of the Legislature in 1945. Named for Andrew Summers Rowan, carrier of the "message to Garcia". The oldest building, erected in 1833, is of Thomas Jefferson design and named in his honor.

WV 3, Sweet Springs

ANN ROYALL/SWEET SPRINGS
Ann Royall, America's first woman journalist, lived here. Widowed at 50, she became an author and prominent figure in national political life. In her newspaper, "Paul Pry", at Washington, she set the style for modern columnists.

Settled by James Moss, 1760. William Lewis bought the site and in 1792 built the inn where he entertained Van Buren, Pierce, Fillmore, and others. Thomas Jefferson designed the main building which was erected in 1833.

WV 3, Sweet Springs

GOV. JOHN FLOYD
Near here is grave of John Floyd, 1783-1837. Governor of Virginia, 1830-1834; champion of the Oregon Country and of States' Rights; leader in the formation of the Whig Party; bitter foe of administration of President Andrew Jackson.

WV 3, at junction with WV 311, near Sweet Springs

GREAT EASTERN DIVIDE
At this point atop the Alleghenies is the geographical feature known as the Great Eastern Divide, a natural barrier from which water flows to the Atlantic Ocean by way of the Jackson and James rivers and to the Gulf of Mexico via the Greenbrier, New, Kanawha, Ohio and Miss. rivers. As part of the Proclamation Line of 1763, it temporarily served to stop further western colonial expansion.

WV 3, 5.1 miles west of Sweet Springs

ANDREW S. ROWAN
Colonel Rowan was born here, April 23, 1857; graduated from West Point, 1881. Famed for securing vital information from Garcia, rebel leader of Cuba, during War with Spain, 1898. For this exploit, he was given the D.S.C. Died, Jan. 11, 1943.

WV 3, Gap Mills

REHOBOTH CHURCH
Indians were still about when Rehoboth Church was dedicated by Bishop Asbury in 1786, and rifles as well as Bibles were carried by the worshipers. This is the oldest church building west of the Allegheny Mountains.

WV 3, 2 miles east of Union

In 1960, Rehoboth Church was designated one of ten Methodist Shrines in America.

FIRST CORN CLUB

West Virginia's first Corn Club was organized at Pickaway School on idea of county superintendent C.A. Keadle, with support from WVU Agricultural Dean T.C. Atkenson. WVU Extension Dept. provided 71 schoolchildren with tested seed in 1908 and 46 entered crop in corn show at courthouse in Union in November. Corn Clubs, later known as Agricultural Clubs, paved the way for today's 4-H Clubs.

US 219, near junction with WV 3, Pickaway

JOSEPH SWOPE

Born 1707 in Germany, Swope came to America ca. 1720. Reputedly first to settle Monroe County, ca. 1752, when part of Augusta Co. Son Michael, born 29 Sept. 1753, recorded as 1st white child born in Monroe. Nearby is grave of son Joseph, seized in 1756 Shawnee raid and held captive for nine years. Swope served in Colonial Wars and his sons, Joseph, John and Michael served in the American Revolution.

WV 3, near Wolf Creek

REFORMATORY FOR WOMEN

The only Federal industrial institution for women is one mile west. Established by an act of Congress, June 7, 1924. Received first tenants, April 30, 1927. Formally opened Nov. 24, 1928. Stresses rehabilitation and industrial education.

WV 3, Alderson (Monroe County)

CIVIL WAR MONUMENT

On Aug. 21, 1901 this 20 ft. monument with 6 ft. statue depicting typical Confederate soldier was dedicated to the Monroe County men who served the lost cause. Hinton Marble Works produced the Italian marble statue, standing on granite pedestal placed on native blue limestone. Site selected in anticipation of Union's growth. Dedication crowd of 10,000 heard speech of Gen. John Echols.

US 219, near Union Presbyterian Church, Union

GENERAL JOHN ECHOLS

Gen. Echols was born March 20, 1823 in Lynchburg, Virginia. He entered the Confederate Army from his home in Union. With rank of Lieut. Col., Echols commanded the 27th Virginia Brigade, Staunton Infantry, at Manassas and was severely wounded at Kernstown. He was commissioned Brig. Gen. on April 16, 1862. His later service was mostly in West Virginia. He died May 24, 1896 and was buried in Staunton.

US 219, courthouse square, Union

UNION

Settled in 1774 by James Alexander, who later served in Revolutionary Army. County organized at his house, 1799. "Walnut Grove," built by Andrew Beirne, and "Elmwood," built by the Capertons, fine examples of colonial architecture.

US 219, courthouse square, Union

BISHOP MATTHEW W. CLAIR, SR.

Born at Union, 1865. Converted at 15 at Simpson M.E. Church, Charleston. Licensed to preach; his first parish was Harpers Ferry, 1889. His most distinguished pastoral work was the rebuilding of Asbury Church, Washington, with a seating capacity of 1800. He was one of the two first Negroes in Methodism to achieve the office of bishop. He died in Covington, Ky., in 1943, and was buried in Washington, D.C.

WV 3, near US 219, Union

BIG LIME

The Greenbrier Limestone, which outcrops along U.S. Route 219 between here and Renick, is the "Big Lime" of the driller. Fish-egg like oölitic zones in the "Big Lime" yield oil and natural gas in West Virginia.

US 219, 1 mile south of Union

SALT SULPHUR

Opened as a resort in 1820. Main building erected about 1836. Martin Van Buren, Clay, and Calhoun among prominent guests. General Jenkins and other Confederate leaders made headquarters here during several campaigns.

US 219, 2 miles south of Union

BLOCK HOUSE ON INDIAN CREEK/ HOME OF ISAAC ESTILL

Built by Wallace Estill, who relocated here in fall 1773 from Fort George on Bullpasture R. He was comm. Capt. in 1752, served in Colonial Wars against Native Americans; and as High Sheriff & Magistrate, Augusta Co. 3-story stone home with 18 in. walls, served as block house for protection against raids. Capt. Estill died, 1792, age 94. Son, Isaac, inherited and likely added frame addition. Placed on National Register in 1984.

Isaac moved to block house on Indian Creek in 1773 at age 7 with Wallace & Mary Ann Campbell Estill. In 1788 he married Elizabeth, dau. of John Frogg, killed in 1774 at Battle of Pt. Pleasant & granddau. of John Lewis, 1st settler of Augusta Co. Isaac served in 1799 as 1st and later 6th sheriff of Monroe Co.; in Va General Assembly, 1806-09 and 1817-18; and as a Major in the Virginia Militia. Relocated to Kentucky in 1818.

WV 122, 0.9 miles west of junction with US 219

SALTPETER CAVES

The large rooms of these caves have high vaults and are easily accessible from the outside and are dry under foot. They were owned by John Maddy in 1804. He sold them to Jacob and John Mann who manufactured saltpeter here for several years. The caves were used for the same purpose during Civil War. Old wooden hoppers still stand and mule tracks can yet be seen on the long walkways where the wagons used to run.

WV 122, just east of Greenville

COOK'S FORT

Cook's Fort on Indian Creek was a strong defensive post. It covered over an acre of ground and sheltered 300 people during the Indian invasion of 1778. Near the fort several settlers were killed by the savages.

WV 122, just west of Greenville

GRAVE OF ELIZABETH GRAHAM STODGHILL

Atop the hill on the Coulter farm is the gravesite of Elizabeth Graham Stodghill (1770-1858), and her husband Joel. In 1777, at the age of 7, Elizabeth was captured by a band of Shawnees who raided her home at Lowell and took her to Ohio. She was found and ransomed by her father, James Graham Sr., in 1785. Gravesite located, 1973, by Carrie Reardon, nee Graham, great-great-great granddaughter of the Lowell homesteader.

US 219, just north of Lindside

WOODS' FORT

This defense, erected, 1773, by Captain Michael Woods, was of importance during Lord Dunmore's War. Troops from here were engaged in the Battle of Point Pleasant next year and later were with George Rogers Clark.

US 219, north of Peterstown

PETERSTOWN

Founded by Christian Peters who settled two miles east, 1784. Established as a town, 1804. Peters was an expert rifleman in the Revolutionary Army and took part in several battles. Descendants live in home of his son, built in 1812.

*US 219, Peterstown

HOME OF THE JONES DIAMOND

An alluvial diamond weighing 34.48 carats, largest to date found in America, was discovered here in April 1928, by William P. "Punch" Jones and his father, Grover C. Jones, Sr., while pitching horseshoes in the home yard of Mr. and Mrs. Grover C. Jones. "Punch" was later killed in combat during World War II. Mr. and Mrs. Grover C. Jones still retain ownership of the diamond.

Sycamore Street, at junction with Jones Street, Peterstown

RED SULPHUR SPRINGS

Site of a popular resort hotel, built in 1832. Water from the springs was reputed to have curative value. Hotel was used as a military hospital during Civil War. Last owner was Levi P. Morton, vice-president under Benjamin Harrison.

WV 12, Red Sulphur Springs

MORGAN COUNTY

Formed, 1820, from Berkeley and Hampshire. Named for Gen. Daniel Morgan of the Revolutionary Army. Many of his renowned "Riflemen" were from the Eastern Panhandle, where he once lived. Famed Berkeley Springs here.

WV 9, Morgan-Berkeley border; *WV 9 West, Morgan-Hampshire border; *WV 9 East, Morgan-Hampshire border; *WV 9, Morgan-Maryland border

"STONEWALL" JACKSON HILL

From this point, "Stonewall" Jackson shelled Hancock, Md., Jan. 5, 1862. After destroying supplies, the B&O track and the bridge over the Great Cacapon, Jackson marched his army of 8,500 men to Romney and captured it, January 14.

US 522, Morgan-Maryland border

ORISKANY SAND

The pure massive sandstone forming Warm Springs Ridge is the Oriskany of the driller and geologist. The "Oriskany Sand", an important gas sand, has produced in excess of a trillion cubic feet of gas in West Virginia.

*US 522, 2 miles north of Berkeley Springs

LOVERS' LEAP

Beautiful panorama of West Virginia, Pennsylvania, and Maryland.

It overlooks the Chesapeake and Ohio Canal which was started by George Washington and associates in order to improve communication with the West.

US 522, north of Berkeley Springs

BERKELEY SPRINGS/ JAMES RUMSEY

Washington first came here, 1748. Fairfax gave the springs to the public. Established as town, 1776. Virginia treated her sick soldiers here. Gen. Washington, Gen. Buchanan, Gen. Gates, Charles Carroll, and others bought lots, 1777.

Here, 1782-1785, lived James Rumsey, miller, innkeeper, and inventor of the steamboat. He demonstrated a model of his boat before Washington, 1784. He continued his experiments here and elsewhere

James Rumsey

until his public demonstration of 1787.

US 522 (S. Washington Street), at junction with Fairfax Street, Berkeley Springs

BERKELEY SPRINGS SANITARIUM

These healing springs, visited by Washington, 1748, were given to Virginia by Lord Fairfax. Helpful in

Lithograph of the pavilion at Berkeley Springs, circa 1850

treating infantile paralysis, rheumatism, diabetes, and other diseases. Temperature of water is always 74 degrees.

US 522, Berkeley Springs State Park, Berkeley Springs

CENTENNIAL TIME CAPSULE
This official West Virginia Centennial Time Capsule was dedicated October 12, 1963 as Morgan County's contribution to the State's Centennial celebration. It contains historical documents, personal messages to be distributed in 2063.

US 522, Berkeley Springs State Park, Berkeley Springs

J.H. Diss Debar sketch of author David Hunter Strother, "Porte Crayon," during the Civil War

"PORTE CRAYON"
Home of Gen. David Hunter Strother, soldier, writer, traveler, and artist. He used the pen name, "Porte Crayon." Washington Irving, his friend, wrote much of his "Life of Washington" in the Strother study.

US 522, Berkeley Springs

COOLFONT MANOR HOUSE
Directional Marker: Approach to Coolfont Manor House, once the home of Herbert Quick, internationally famous novelist, agronomist and friend of U.S. Presidents. Now home of the non-profit Coolfont Foundation, for the promotion of the arts.

WV 9, Berkeley Springs

SIR JOHN'S RUN
Sir John's Run was named for Sir John Sinclair, the quartermaster for General Braddock on expedition in 1755 against the French at Fort Duquesne. James Rumsey demonstrated his steamboat here in 1785.

WV 9, west of Berkeley Springs

PROSPECT PEAK
This headland overlooks the Potomac and Great Cacapon Valleys and the three states—West Virginia, Pennsylvania, and Maryland. The National Geographic Magazine rates this scene among America's outstanding beauty spots.

WV 9, 3 miles west of Berkeley Springs

TUSCARORA (CLINTON) SAND

The massive resistant Tuscarora Sandstone is steeply inclined here and forms Fluted Rocks. The "Tuscarora (Clinton) Sand" of the driller produces some gas although it is largely untested in West Virginia.

WV 9, 3 miles west of Berkeley Springs

ORISKANY SAND

The pure massive sandstone quarried for glass manufacture on Warm Springs Ridge is the Oriskany of the driller and geologist. The "Oriskany Sand", an important gas Sand, has produced in excess of a trillion cubic feet of gas in West Virginia.

Off US 522, on road to lodge, Cacapon Resort State Park

PAW PAW

Important concentration point of the Union Army from 1861 to 1865. As many as 16,000 Federal troops were encamped here at one time. A blockhouse stood along tracks of the B&O Railroad at this point.

WV 9, Paw Paw

NICHOLAS COUNTY

Formed in 1818 from Greenbrier, Kanawha and Randolph. Named for Wilson C. Nicholas, governor, Virginia, 1814-1817. In this county in 1861 sharp engagements were fought at Kessler's Cross Lanes and at Carnifex Ferry.

*US 19, Nicholas-Braxton border; WV 16, Nicholas-Clay border; *US 19, Nicholas-Fayette border; *WV 39, Nicholas-Fayette border; WV 20, Nicholas-Greenbrier border; WV 39, Nicholas-Greenbrier border; *WV 20, Nicholas-Webster border*

"CRUPPERNECK BEND"

Scenic view of Gauley River which rises in Pocahontas County at elevation of 4100 feet and flows southwesterly to join New River, forming Great Kanawha. Cranberry, Cherry, Meadow, Williams Rivers are its tributaries.

WV 20/WV 55, 2.2 miles south of split, Craigsville

LEIVASY

The village of Leivasy, formerly known as Meadowvale, was established with post office and general store Oct. 3, 1879. Valentine Leivasy was the first postmaster and merchant. Surnames of early settlers include Bennett, Callison, Davis, Journelle, McClung, McCutcheon, Nicholas, Odell, Pittsenberger, White and Williams. A centennial celebration held Oct. 6, 1979, drew an estimated 4000 people.

WV 20, Leivasy

SUMMERSVILLE

Summersville was established in 1820 and made the county seat. Nicholas County, which was settled about 1785, was crossed by the Pocahontas Trail which led from the Greenbrier Valley to the Valley of the Great Kanawha.

WV 41 (Main Street), at junction with Church Street, 0.2 miles north of WV 39, Summersville

NANCY HART'S CAPTURE

Nancy Hart, noted, beautiful Confederate spy, was seized July, 1862, leading attack in which most of Summersville was burned. She killed her guard with his pistol and escaped. She was buried on Manning Knob.

WV 41 (Main Street), at junction with Church Street, 0.2 miles north of WV 39, Summersville

CARNIFEX FERRY

Scene of battle, Sept. 10, 1861, between Federal army of Gen. W.S. Rosecrans and Confederate army of Gen. John B. Floyd. This engagement followed defeat of Federal troops at Cross Lanes, Aug. 26, 1861. State acquired title of site, Oct. 29, 1935.

County Route 23, Carnifex Ferry Battlefield State Park

"Battle of Carnifex Ferry, September 10, 1861." Drawn by J. Nep Roesler of the Color Guard of the 47th Ohio Volunteers. Roesler sketched numerous Civil War scenes in western Virginia, which were printed in the New River War Album (1862).

CROSS LANES BATTLE

Site of the surprise attack by the Confederates under General John B. Floyd on the early morning of Aug. 26, 1861, against Federal troops of the 7th Ohio Inf., led by Colonel E.B. Tyler. The Federal soldiers were badly defeated and scattered. They lost 132 men, including killed and captured. This surprise attack also known as the Battle of Knives and Forks.

WV 129, at junction with County Route 9, Keslers Cross Lanes

ZOAR BAPTIST CHURCH

Organized on April 17, 1824 by twelve members from the Hopewell Church in Fayette County at the home of Henry Morris on Peter's Creek. The first building of frame, constructed in 1840, was destroyed by Union soldiers in 1861. The building was replaced but it burned in 1879. A new church was erected, but it too was destroyed by fire in 1955. The present building was erected in 1955.

WV 129, 0.2 miles west of County Route 9, Keslers Cross Lanes

NORTH AND SOUTH

At Kessler's Cross Lanes (5 Mi. E.), Aug. 26, 1861 and at Carnifex Ferry (7 Mi. E.), Sept. 10, 1861, Battles occurred between Confederates under Gen. J.B. Floyd and Union troops under Col. E.B. Tyler and Gen. W.S. Rosecrans.

WV 39/WV 129, Drennen

MORRIS MASSACRE

Scene of massacre, 1792, of daughters of Henry Morris, early settler and son of first permanent settler in Great Kanawha Valley. Graves of Henry Morris and the Indian victims may be seen from the road.

WV 39, Lockwood

OHIO COUNTY

Formed in 1776 from West Augusta. Named for the river which bears an Indian name meaning "Beautiful River." Scene of last battle of the Revolution, 1782. Visited by La Salle, Celoron, Gist, Washington, and later explorers.

*WV 88, Ohio-Brooke border; *WV 2, Ohio-Brooke border; WV 2, Ohio-Marshall border; WV 88, Ohio-Marshall border; US 40/US 250, Wheeling Island, Ohio-Ohio state border; US 40, Ohio-Pennsylvania border

WEST LIBERTY

First organized town in the Ohio Valley. Formed in 1787. First court of Ohio County met at Black's Cabin here in 1777. Near by is grave of Captain Samuel Brady, hero of the Pennsylvania and Virginia frontiers.

WV 88, West Liberty Elementary School, West Liberty

WEST LIBERTY STATE COLLEGE

Founded by Virginia Assembly, 1837; operated privately, 1838-1870. Became state institution, 1870, with name West Liberty State Normal. Name changed to West Liberty State

Teachers College in 1931 and to West Liberty State College in 1943.

WV 88, West Liberty State College, West Liberty

FORT VAN METER

Fort Van Meter once commanded by Major Samuel McCulloch, the noted Indian fighter, whose heroic deeds are favorite border stories. On a scouting trip with his brother, McCulloch was killed in 1782, and is buried nearby.

WV 88, Clinton (between West Liberty and Wheeling)

RAY'S ARITHMETIC

North, Joseph Ray, who wrote the

celebrated Ray's Arithmetic, was born, Nov. 25, 1807. At the age of 16, Ray went to Cincinnati where in 1834 he published the first of his series of textbooks on arithmetic and algebra.

US 40, Valley Grove

RONEY'S POINT

Here is located the historic "Heimberger House", one of the first and most famous of the numerous stopping places which sprang up to serve the traffic on the National Road. Still standing, it is now called the "Old Stone House".

US 40, Roney's Point, between Valley Grove and Triadelphia near Wheeling

TRIADELPHIA

Named for three friends. Near this spot, on Middle Wheeling Creek, Jonathan Link built a blockhouse in 1780. Next year a band of 20 Indians killed Link and two companions and captured and tomahawked Presley Peak and William Hawkins.

US 40, city hall building, Triadelphia (two markers)

THE NATIONAL PIKE

The National Pike, called the "Old Cumberland Road", was started in 1811 and used to Wheeling in 1817 and by mail coaches from Washington by 1818. Most of it followed the Nemacolin Path and Braddock's Road from Cumberland, Md.

US 40, near entrance to Wheeling Park, Wheeling

JESSE LEE RENO

Major General Jesse Lee Reno was born at Wheeling, June 20, 1823. He served in the Mexican War. He was killed at South Mountain, Maryland, September 14, 1862, while commanding the 9th Army Corps, United States Volunteers. Major General Reno was West Virginia's highest ranking United States officer killed in the Civil War. He is buried in the Oak Hill Cemetery, in Georgetown, Maryland.

US 40, near entrance to Wheeling Park, Wheeling

STATE'S BIRTHPLACE

West Virginia was organized in 1861 at Washington Hall, 12th and Market streets. The Linsly Institute Building, Eoff and 15th Streets, was the first Capitol. From 1875 to 1885, the Capitol was in the County-City Building.

US 40, near entrance to Wheeling Park, Wheeling

GIBSON-LINN

Among many daring frontier exploits was the journey of Captain George Gibson and Lieutenant William Linn to New Orleans, 1776-77. Despite danger and opposition, they secured powder for use of Fort Henry against the Indians.

US 40, Grandview section of Wheeling

MOUNT DE CHANTAL

Established in 1848, it was incorporated as the Wheeling Female Academy in 1852. Founded by the Sisters of the Visitation and the Right Rev. R.V. Whelan, Bishop of Richmond, to educate Catholic women, the academy moved to this location and main building in 1865. Placed on National Register in 1978, it is open to students of all denominations.

Washington Avenue, Wheeling

"MONUMENT PLACE"

On site of Fort Shepherd is this mansion, built in 1798 by Moses Shepherd and known as Shepherd Hall. Among its guests were Lafayette, James K. Polk, Andrew Jackson, and Henry Clay. Clay's support brought National Pike here.

US 40/WV 88, in Elm Grove section of Wheeling

ELM GROVE STONE BRIDGE

Built in 1817 by Moses Shepherd, a prominent Ohio Countian, as part of the National Road. Constructed of uncoursed limestone, but covered by concrete in 1958, it is the oldest extant three span elliptical arch bridge in the state. Also known as "Monument Place Bridge" due to the nearby memorial built to Henry Clay by Shepherd in honor of his support for National Road construction.

US 40, at Little Wheeling Creek in Elm Grove section of Wheeling

FORKS OF WHEELING CREEK

Geo. Washington described the land here in 1770. The French expedition headed by Capt. Celeron buried leaden plates at the mouth in 1749

122

and claimed land for France. De Bonnescamp's map gives creek name—Kanonouaras.

US 40/WV 88, in Elm Grove section of Wheeling

VINEYARD HILLS

Site of 31 acre vineyard owned and operated by Fr. John Peter Kreusch (1818-88), German priest who served St. Alphonsus German Catholic Church (1859-83). Vineyard, set circa 1862, yielded from 4,000 to 15,000 gallons of unadulterated altar wine used by area churches annually until 1890s. Cellars were 80' long, 25' wide and 20' high. Father Kreusch's vineyard was one of several along Ohio River.

989 Grandview Street, near US 40 Wheeling Hill, Wheeling

THE WASHINGTONS

Nearby are buried Lawrence Augustine Washington, his wife, Dorcas, and daughter, Emma Tell. Lawrence was the son of Samuel Washington, youngest brother of General Washington. Part of their original home is standing.

*US 40, near junction with WV 88, in Woodsdale section of Wheeling

WHEELING

Indian word. Settled, 1769, by Ebenezer, Jonathan, Andrew, and Silas Zane. Fort Henry, once Fort Fincastle, built, 1774. Mail boats, 1794, National Pike, 1818, and B.&O. Railroad, 1852, combined with its iron mills to make Wheeling a great manufacturing center.

WV 2, Kossuth Park, near Main Street exit of I-70 East, Wheeling

The second siege of Fort Henry, Wheeling, in 1782 was one of the last battles of the American Revolution. This 1882 painting by Joseph Faris depicts Betty Zane's daring run to retrieve gunpowder.

STATE OF WEST VIRGINIA

WHEELING
SUSPENSION BRIDGE
...

The Wheeling Suspension Bridge, constructed by Charles Ellet, Jr. between 1846 and 1849, was the first long-span wire-cable suspension bridge in the United States. For many years it was the longest clear-span bridge in the world. The deck was wrecked by a violent storm in 1854. It was re-built and the structure with its original towers and cables is still in service. It is the most significant remaining pre-Civil War bridge in the nation.

WEST VIRGINIA DEPARTMENT OF ARCHIVES AND HISTORY, 1975

FORT HENRY/FORT HENRY

Attacked, 1777, by Wyandot, Mingo, and Shawnee Indians who were repulsed by garrison under David Shepherd after white scouting parties had lost heavily. Maj. Samuel McCulloch made famous ride over cliff during attack.

Last battle of the American Revolution fought here, September 11-13, 1782. Ebenezer and Silas Zane led force which defeated British and Indians under British officers, carrying a British flag. Scene of Betty Zane's heroic act.

WV 2 (1000 block of Main Street), Wheeling

WHEELING SUSPENSION BRIDGE

The Wheeling Suspension Bridge, constructed by Charles Ellet, Jr. between 1846 and 1849, was the first long-span wire-cable suspension bridge in the United States. For many years it was the longest clear-span bridge in the world. The deck was wrecked by a violent storm in 1854. It was re-built and the structure with its original towers and cables is still in service. It is the most significant remaining pre-Civil War bridge in the nation.

WV 2 (10th and Main streets), Wheeling

OLD CUSTOM HOUSE

Designed by federal architect Ammi B. Young for use as Custom House, Post Office and Federal Court. Constructed 1856-9 at cost of $96,918. Convention here in 1861 helped set stage for West Virginia Statehood. State's first constitution approved here in 1862. Arthur Boreman, first Governor, and other officials, had offices here through 1863 when control returned to U.S. Government.

West Virginia Independence Hall, 16th and Market streets, Wheeling

CAMP CARLISLE

At this camp, Generals Duval, Kelley, and Colonel Thoburn recruited and rendezvoused the First (West) Virginia Inf., Volunteers. Later, name was changed to Camp Willey, in honor of one of the State's first United States Senators.

*Zane and North Wabash streets on Wheeling Island, Wheeling

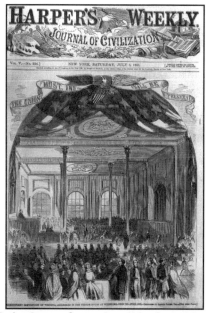

Artist Jasper Green drew this view of the interior of the Custom House during the second Wheeling Convention in June 1861.

PENDLETON COUNTY

Formed in 1788 from Hardy, Augusta, Rockingham. Named for Edmund Pendleton, Virginia statesman-jurist. This county has a range of altitude of over 3500 feet. Here are Seneca Rocks, Smoke Hole, and Spruce Knob.

WV 28, Pendleton-Grant border; US 220, Pendleton-Grant border; WV 28, Pendleton-Pocahontas border; US 33, Pendleton-Randolph border

OLD JUDY CHURCH

Oldest log church building in Pendleton Co. Built in 1848 of hewn white pine logs cut nearby. Served as Methodist Episcopal Church until 1910 when abandoned. Used as community center since rededication in 1936.

US 220, 100 yards south of Grant-Pendleton border

SMOKE HOLE

The Smoke Hole, a rugged canyon of 1421 feet elevation, made by the South Branch of the Potomac River, extends eighteen miles to the junction with the North Fork. In Coeymans Limestone of Devonian Age, the river has carved out various formations and caves. Big Cave and Old Mines Cave, where saltpeter was made during the War Between the States, are the most noted. Smoke Hole is one of the State's natural wonders.

US 220, about 1 mile north of County Route 2 (Smoke Hole Road), near Upper Tract

SMOKE HOLE

Smoke Hole, a rugged canyon formed by the South Branch of the Potomac River, extends eighteen miles south to U.S. 220. Early explorers reported that heavy mists rising from the canyon looked like smoke coming from a deep hole. The canyon contains many caves and spectacular rock formations. Among the many caves is Smoke Hole Cave. Its name originates from the presence of smoke stains on the roof which may have been caused by Indian campfires.

County Route 2 (Smoke Hole Road), at junction with US 220, near Upper Tract

EAGLE ROCKS

Named for William Eagle, a Revolutionary War soldier who lived nearby. Enlisting at age fifteen, 12-24-1776, he served in the 3rd, 4th, 8th, and 12th Va. Rgts., Continental Line, at Valley Forge and Yorktown. Died, 1848, and is buried here.

County Route 2 (Smoke Hole Road), two miles from junction with US 220

SMOKE HOLE CAVE

On Smoke Hole Knob (300 yards west), overlooking this site, is Smoke Hole Cave with its circular chamber, forty feet high and fifteen feet in diameter, resembling an inverted hornet's nest, tapering to a natural chimney or "smoke hole". Its use by

Indian tribes and early settlers as a place to "smoke cure" meats gave the name of Smoke Hole to the cave and to this twenty-mile picturesque canyon.

*County Route 2, 4 miles from junction with US 220

ST. GEORGE'S CHURCH
Built about 1850 as Methodist Episcopal Meeting House and known as Palestine Church. First trustees: Alfred Kimble, Jacob L. Kimble, J.H. Lantz, Abraham Kile, and Isaac Ault. Bought by Episcopal Church, 1931; rededicated, 1966.

County Route 2 (Smoke Hole Road), five miles from junction with US 220

FORT UPPER TRACT
Site of Fort Upper Tract, one of the forts erected under Washington's orders to guard the settlements. In 1758, Indians captured and burned it. Captain James Dunlap and 21 others were killed. No one escaped.

US 220, Upper Tract

FORT SEYBERT
Fort Seybert, strong frontier post with blockhouse, cabins, and stockade, surrendered to the Indians after three-day siege in 1758. Twenty of the prisoners were massacred and the others were carried into captivity. (Site 2 Mi. North)

US 33, at junction with County Route 3 (Sweedlin Valley Road), Oak Flat

PROPST LUTHERAN CHURCH
61 rods west stood original round log church upon 3 1/2 acre plot deeded Dec. 18, 1769, by John Michael Propst and his wife Catherine, "for the congregation of the South Fork of the Potowmack for five shillings current money of Virginia."

County Route 21, just north of junction with County Route 21/9 (Hively Gap Road), 2 miles south of Brandywine

TROUT ROCK FORT
The Trout Rock Fort was one in the chain of forts that the Virginia House of Burgesses in March 1756 directed Washington to erect for the defense of settlers in the South Branch Valley. It also marks the end of Gen. Stonewall Jackson's pursuit of the Federals after the Battle of McDowell, May 12, 1862. On this site during the War Between the States, gunpowder was made from saltpeter obtained in a nearby cave.

US 220, 4 miles south of Franklin

DEVONIAN SHALE
The carbonaceous shale exposed in the quarry is the Marcellus brown and black shale of the driller. It yields large amounts of natural gas in southern West Virginia.

US 220, 2 miles south of Franklin

FRANKLIN
Settled, 1769. Named for its founder, Francis Evick. John Van Meter first reached the South Branch, 1725. Roger Dyer and others came about

1745. Site of Federal camp of Gen. John C. Fremont, 1862, on way to attack "Stonewall" Jackson.

US 220, courthouse square, Franklin

CRAGS—CAVERNS
Northwest: Seneca Rocks, overlooking old Seneca Trail or Warriors' Path; Champe Rocks; Germany Valley and Seneca Caverns. West: Spruce Knob and Spruce Lake. East: Shenandoah Mountains. Northeast: the Smoke Hole.

*US 33, North Fork Mountain, between Franklin and Judy Gap

GERMANY VALLEY
In Germany Valley is the site of Hinkle's Fort built in 1761-1762. It was the only defense of the South Branch after Fort Upper Tract and Fort Seybert were destroyed by

Shawnee Indians under Killbuck, April 27-28, 1758.

US 33, North Fork Mountain, 4 miles south of junction with WV 28, between Franklin and Judy Gap

BIRTHPLACE OF RIVERS
Here mountain waters divide into many rivers. Greenbrier, Gauley, and Elk start south and west to the Kanawha; the Jackson east to the James; north goes the South Branch to the Potomac, and the Cheat and Tygart to the Monongahela.

WV 28, Pendleton-Pocahontas border

SPRUCE KNOB
Spruce Knob (9 miles W.), 4,860 feet and the highest point in West Virginia, lies slightly above the crest ridge of Spruce Mountain. The crest lies above 4,500 feet for more than

Scene from Franklin, Pendleton County, after a 1924 fire

GERMANY VALLEY

In Germany Valley is the site of Hinkle's Fort built in 1761-1762. It was the only defense of the South Branch after Fort Upper Tract and Fort Seybert were destroyed by Shawnee Indians under Killbuck. April 27-28. 1758.

10 miles and is strewn with fragments of Pottsville Sandstone of the Pennsylvanian Age. Nearby are Spruce Lake and the Sinks, where the Gandy Creek disappears for about a mile into a cavern beneath a spur of the Alleghenies.

US 33 and secondary road 33/4 (Spruce Knob Road) near Judy Gap

ORISKANY SAND

The massive sandstone across the road is the Oriskany of the driller and geologist. The "Oriskany Sand", an important gas sand, has produced in excess of a trillion cubic feet of gas in West Virginia.

*US 33, WV 28 at junction with County Route 9 (Germany Valley Road-Dolly Hills Road), Riverton; *US 33, at Hively Gap, near Franklin*

GRAVESITE OF JOHN DOLLY

Nearby is grave of John Dolly (Dahle, 1749-1847), a Hessian mercenary in the Revolutionary War and an early settler in Germany Valley. Naming of Dolly Sods attributed to his surname and large tracts of grass sod lands found here.

County Route 9/4 (Horse Ridge), off County Route 9 (Germany Valley-Dolly Hills Road), near Riverton

SENECA ROCKS

Seneca Rocks, an outstanding natural formation, rises over 900 feet high, overlooking the junction of the Seneca and Shawnee trails or Warriors' Path and the site of an Indian village with its legend of "Snow Bird", the Indian Princess. The almost perpendicular strata are of Tuscarora Sandstone of the Silurian Age.

US 33 and WV 28/WV 55, Seneca Rocks

Seneca Rocks

TUSCARORA (CLINTON) SAND

The massive vertical sandstone forming Judy Rocks is the Tuscarora of the driller and geologist. The "Tuscarora (Clinton) Sand" yields some gas although it is largely untested in West Virginia.

US 33, at junction with WV 28

TUSCARORA (CLINTON) SAND

The vertical resistant sandstone forming Seneca Rocks is the Tuscarora of the driller and geologist. The "Tuscarora Sand" yields some gas although it is largely untested in West Virginia.

*US 33 and WV 28/WV 55, Seneca Rocks

CHAMPE ROCKS

Near Champe Rocks is the home and grave of Sergeant John Champe who was sent by General Washington and Major Lee to kidnap Benedict Arnold, the traitor, from within the British lines. The daring plot almost succeeded.

WV 28/WV 55, approximately 5 miles north of Mouth of Seneca

PLEASANTS COUNTY

Formed in 1851 from Wood, Tyler and Ritchie. Named for James Pleasants, governor of Virginia, 1822-1825. County's early development was due to resources of oil and natural gas. St. Marys, county seat, founded, 1849, by A.H. Creel.

WV 16, Pleasants-Ritchie border; *WV 2, Pleasants-Tyler border; *WV 2, Pleasants-Wood border; WV 2, Pleasants-Ohio state border

EARLY SETTLERS

In 1790, the La Rue brothers, Frenchmen, built homes in Pleasants County. Isaac settled on Middle Island Creek. Jacob had a home on Middle Island and a mill on Broad Run. Graves of his family are on Middle Island.

WV 2, St. Marys

ST. MARYS

Established as a town, 1851, by Alexander H. Creel on land originally granted to Henry Thomas, Revolutionary soldier, in 1785. Creel built the "Cain House", which became one of the most famous of the Ohio River taverns.

WV 2, St. Marys

VAUCLUSE

Named for the French town which was made famous by the poet, Petrarch. It was established in 1837 by Alexander H. Creel and was the business center of a large area until St. Marys became the county seat.

*WV 2, near St. Marys

COW RUN SAND

The pebbly Saltsburg Sandstone, the "Cow Run Sand" of the driller, is brought to the surface by the sharp upwarp of the Burning Springs (Volcano) Anticline. The "Sand" yields oil and natural gas at depths of over 400 feet on both flanks of the Anticline.

*WV 2, near Belmont

St. Marys

HENDERSON HOME

Home built by Alexander Henderson in 1814. He and his brother settled about 1798 on land granted their father in 1783. One of the Hendersons, a seaman, brought peaches from Portugal to start fruit industry here.

WV 2, Willow Island

POCAHONTAS COUNTY

Formed from Bath, Pendleton and Randolph in 1821. Named for Pocahontas, Indian princess, friend of the Jamestown settlers. Site of Droop Mountain battle, November 6, 1863. The famous Cranberry Glades are in this county.

*WV 39, Pocahontas-Greenbrier border; US 219, Pocahontas-Greenbrier border (two markers); WV 28, Pocahontas-Pendleton border; US 219, Pocahontas-Randolph border; US 250, Pocahontas-Randolph border; *WV 84, Pocahontas-Virginia border*

CAMP ALLEGHENY

Confederate forces led by Col. Edward Johnson held a fortified camp here in winter of 1861-62. Sharp attack occurred, Dec. 13, 1861, in which the Union troops under Gen. Robert Milroy were beaten off.

US 250, West Virginia-Virginia border

BLUE AND GRAY/ "TRAVELERS REPOSE"

Near here was Camp Bartow, fortified by Confederates in 1861. At Greenbrier Bridge, an artillery duel was fought, Oct. 3, 1861. Battle of Allegheny (8 Mi. E.) was fought, Dec. 13, 1861, between armies of Gen. W.L. Jackson and Gen. R.L. Milroy.

Cass Scenic Railroad State Park features rides on the steam-driven locomotives originally used to haul lumber to the mill at Cass.

A Pocahontas County limestone quarry, date unknown

Made famous in novels of Hergesheimer, Bierce, and others. This is the country of "Tol'able David". On the neighboring hills are the Confederate trenches guarding their camp in 1861, near which several battles were fought.

US 250/WV 28, Bartow

CASS

Town developed by Sam E. Slaymaker, representative of the W.Va. Spruce Lumber Company who leased 200,000 acres of timber land here in 1899. With the efforts of Italian immigrant labor, the town, a band-saw mill, and eleven miles of railroad were completed by 1902. Named for Joseph K. Cass, chairman of the Board of the W.Va. Pulp and Paper company, which owned the operation until its sale to the Dan Mower Lumber Company in 1942.

Reduced profits led to the closing of the mill in 1960 and the decline of the town. State purchased in 1963 to operate scenic railroad, and acquired town and remaining Mower tract in 1977.

WV 66, Cass Scenic Railroad State Park, Cass

LEE'S HEADQUARTERS

On this knoll, General Robert E. Lee maintained headquarters from July to September, 1861, after taking command of the Confederate forces in West Virginia. His army on Valley Mountain guarded the road leading south into Virginia.

US 219/WV 55, 0.1 miles north of junction with WV 66

BIG LIME

The Greenbrier Limestone, in this quarry is the "Big Lime" of the driller. Fish-egg like oölitic zones in the "Big Lime" yield oil and natural gas in West Virginia.

US 219, 0.5 miles north of junction with County Route 1 (Back Mountain Road)

EDRAY
Site of early settlement and fort of Thomas Drinnon. Scene of attacks by Indians in 1774 and 1778. To the east, on the land of Jacob Warwick, stood Fort Clover Lick, garrisoned during the Revolutionary War by Augusta County militia.

US 219, at junction with County Route 1 (Back Mountain Road)

MARLINTON/MARLINTON
The old Seneca Indian Trail from New York to Georgia may be seen at this point. During the French and Indian War, 18 settlers lost lives in vicinity. During Indian raids in 1779, 13 were killed and many were taken captive.

Settled, 1749, by Sewell and Marlin. The oldest recorded settlement on western waters. Here stood oak, marking corner of first survey west of Alleghenies. Here was Fort Greenbrier, built, 1755, and garrisoned by Andrew Lewis.

US 219, at junction with County Route 19 (Jerico Road), 0.3 miles south of WV 39, Marlinton

HUNTERSVILLE
Established in 1821. Early trading post here brought hunters and trappers and gave name to the town. In 1822, first county court met here at the home of John Bradshaw. Gen. Lee was encamped here in 1861.

WV 39, 0.9 miles east of WV 28, Huntersville

HUNTERSVILLE JAIL/ PRESBYTERIAN CHURCH
Huntersville was the county seat of Pocahontas, 1821-1891. Jail was built about 1878 of white Medina sandstone and considered almost an escape-proof structure. It was used until county seat was moved to Marlinton in 1891.

The Huntersville Presbyterian Church of colonial style with balcony for slaves was built, 1854, and used by all denominations. Used as hospital and garrison for Confederate and Union troops. Masonic Hall added, 1896, as second story.

WV 39, 0.8 miles east of WV 28, Huntersville

TUSCARORA (CLINTON) SAND
This miniature anticline or upfold (Huntersville Arch) in the Tuscarora Sandstone shows the features of the larger structures which produce oil and gas. The "Tuscarora Sand" produces some gas although it is largely unexplored in West Virginia.

WV 39, 1.8 miles west of WV 92, 1.7 miles east of WV 28, east of Huntersville

RIDER GAP
In this mountain gap, through which came early pioneers, General W.W. Loring camped, 1861, with

10,000 Confederates. In July, General Robert E. Lee succeeded him. North and south is the mountain road which offers a remarkable sky line drive.

WV 39, Valley Mountain

CRANBERRY GLADES

The Cranberry Glades are the naturalist's paradise. In a great natural bowl in nearby mountains, 4000 ft. high, is a misplaced tract of Arctic tundra in southern mountains. Here is found reindeer moss and other rare plants.

WV 39, at entrance to Cranberry Glades Botanical Area Visitor Center, 0.6 miles west of junction with WV 150

MILL POINT

Here in 1750 Stephen Sewell, a pioneer settler, camped. It was site of Fort Day, 1774. To the north James and John Bridger were killed in the Indian raids, 1778. Here James E.A. Gibbs invented the chain stitch sewing machine.

US 219, at junction with WV 39/WV 55, Mill Point

BIRTHPLACE OF PEARL S. BUCK

Pearl Sydenstricker Buck, author of 85 books, one of them "The Good Earth," for which she was awarded the Pulitzer Prize for Literature (1932), was born here at the Stulting Place, June 26, 1892. In 1938, she achieved further distinction when she became the first American woman to receive the Nobel Prize for Literature, based on her six books

Pearl S. Buck, circa 1960s

on China. She died March 6, 1973 and was buried in Bucks County, Pennsylvania.

US 219, 0.7 miles north of County Routes 29 and 31, Hillsboro

HILLSBORO

Here Gen. W.W. Averell camped before the Battle of Droop Mountain and after his raid to Salem, Virginia, in 1863. Settlements were made in the vicinity in the 1760's by John McNeel and the Kinnisons. Birthplace of Pearl Buck.

US 219, 0.3 miles north of County Routes 29 and 31, Hillsboro

DENMAR STATE HOSPITAL

Established in 1938 as Denmar Sanitarium for the tuberculotic colored people. Changed by act of the Leg-

Denmar State Hospital, shown here in the 1960s, has been used as a state correctional facility since 1993.

islature in 1957 to Denmar State Hospital for the chronically ill. Situated 2,200 feet above sea level, it overlooks the Greenbrier River.

County Route 31 (Denmar Road), 4.4 miles south of US 219, Denmar

DROOP MOUNTAIN

Here, November 6, 1863, Union troops, commanded by Gen. W.W. Averell, defeated Confederate forces under Gen. John Echols. This has been considered the most extensive engagement in this State and the site was made a State park in 1929.

US 219, 0.2 miles north of entrance to Droop Mountain State Park

MAXON SAND

The clean massive Droop Sandstone in the road cut is the "Maxon Sand"

of the driller. The "Maxon Sand" yields oil and natural gas at depths of over 1000 feet in southern and central West Virginia.

US 219, just north of Pocahontas-Greenbrier border, 0.1 miles north of junction with County Route 219/11 (Beartown State Park Road)

PRESTON COUNTY

Formed from Monongalia in 1818 and named for James Preston, 13th governor of Virginia. Here is model Federal homestead project, sponsored by Mrs. Eleanor Roosevelt, the wife of Franklin Delano Roosevelt, 32nd President.

*WV 92, Preston-Barbour border; *WV 7, Preston-Monongalia border; County Route 73, Preston-Monongalia border; US*

50, Preston-Taylor border; WV 72, Preston-Tucker border; *US 219, Preston-Tucker border; US 50, Preston-Maryland border; US 219, Preston-Maryland border; *WV 7, Preston-Maryland border; *WV 26, Preston-Pennsylvania border

OLD STONE TAVERN
Built by Henry Grimes circa 1825. It was opened as a tavern in 1841 and kept by George G. Houser, Hiram Hanshaw and William H. Grimes. This was the first tavern in Union District on the Northwestern Turnpike.

US 50, Brookside

SALT SANDS
The massive Homewood Sandstone forming the crest of Laurel Mountain is the "Salt Sand" of the driller. The "Salt Sand" produces oil and natural gas in West Virginia.

US 50, near Aurora

AURORA
Rev. John Stough and family settled at Mount Carmel about 1787, and about 1790 Stough started the first gristmill. The first church was the Salem Evangelical Lutheran Church, organized between 1792 and 1796.

US 50, 0.1 miles east of County Route 53, Aurora

GANTZ SAND
The upper Devonian or lower Mississippian strata and the "Gantz" or "Berea Sand" of the driller, is a clean pebbly sandstone. It produces oil and natural gas at depths greater than 1700 feet in north central West Virginia.

US 50, at entrance to Aurora School, Aurora

B&O VIADUCTS
To S on B&O Railroad is Buckeye Run Viaduct, 136' high, 350' long & 28' wide. Tray Run Viaduct, .6 mi. NW is 148' high, 445' long and 28' wide. Noted engineers Benjamin Latrobe & Albert Fink designed the viaducts. Built 1852 to carry main line, the bridges were reinforced in 1880s & 1900. A Confederate force attacked these key points on the militarily important B&O railroad in April 1863.

WV 72, 0.6 miles north of Rowlesburg

MASON-DIXON LINE
Made famous as line between free and slave states before War Between the States. The survey establishing Maryland-Pennsylvania boundary began, 1763; halted by Indian wars, 1767; continued to southwest corner, 1782; marked, 1784.

WV 26, Preston-Pennsylvania border

WASHINGTON'S CAMP
In 1784 George Washington, Bushrod Washington, James Craik and his son made a horseback journey to inspect their western lands and investigate the feasibility of building a canal from the Potomac River to westward waters. On their return trip, they camped for a night near the present site of Hopemont

Workers pose in front of a B&O Railroad tunnel in Preston County, circa 1900.

before continuing southward through the South Branch Valley and east to Rockingham, Va.

WV 7 at roadside park, 2.5 miles west of West Virginia-Maryland border, Hopemont

HOPEMONT STATE HOSPITAL
Established in 1911 by an act of the Legislature as the State Tuberculosis Sanitarium. In 1921, name was changed to the Hopemont Sanitarium and to the Hopemont State Hospital for the chronically ill, aged, and infirm in 1965.

WV 7, 2.7 miles west of West Virginia-Maryland border, Hopemont

TERRA ALTA
Half a mile high. Famed as a health resort. Once known as Cranberry for extensive cranberry glades found near. North is Cranesville Swamp, noted for its wild life. In that vicinity, Lewis Wetzel killed several Indians.

WV 7, Terra Alta

DR. LOOMIS' GRAVE
In the cemetery is buried Dr. Mahlon Loomis, sender of first aerial signals, 1866-73, forerunner of wireless telegraphy. Signals were sent 14 miles, using kites flown by copper wires. Patented 1872; company chartered by Congress, 1873.

WV 7, west of Terra Alta

ALBRIGHT
Near site of Butler's Fort, built before 1774. Here are the Muddy Creek Park and the sites of Samuel Crane's early gristmill, built on land

Dr. Mahlon Loomis

patented in 1787, and Virginia Iron Furnace, built by Harrison Hagans in 1852.

*WV 26, Albright

OLD IRON FURNACE

Built by Harrison Hagans in 1852. This furnace and others were used to cast iron in frontier days. Early castings were made here for the Brandonville stove used by the early settlers west of the Ohio River.

*WV 26, northwest of Albright

BRANDONVILLE

Made famous by Brandonville stoves, product of old iron furnaces. Here in 1839 was published one of the early agricultural papers. In the vicinity stood Fort Morris, built before 1774 on the lands of Richard Morris.

WV 26, Brandonville

BRUCETON

John Judy and James Clark settled in this vicinity, 1769. First known as Milford for Morton's Mill, built in 1792. The Greenville Iron Furnace,

built about 1815 by Walter Carlile, and the Valley Iron Furnace were not far away.

WV 26, Bruceton Mills

DUNKARD BOTTOM

Thomas Echarlin (Echarly) and two brothers settled here, 1754; first white men of record in Preston County. Brothers killed by Indians and cabin was burned. Site of National Guard Camp since 1909.

WV 7, 1.8 miles east of junction with WV 26

KINGWOOD

Named for grove of big trees. Southeast is Dunkard Bottom, settled by Thomas Eckarly, 1754. Near by during Indian raids in 1778 and 1788, many settlers were killed. Martin Wetzel and William Morgan, noted frontier scouts, had narrow escapes.

WV 7, Kingwood

PRICE'S TAVERN

Preston County was formed in the east upstairs bedroom of Price's Tavern in April, 1818, and named for James Patton Preston, governor of Virginia, 1816-1819. Tavern built prior to 1810, served as an inn until 1882.

WV 7, Kingwood

COW RUN SAND

The massive sandstone, the "Cow Run Sand" of the driller, is the Saltsburg Sandstone and was used in construction near here. It produces oil and natural gas at depths

Bruceton Mills, date unknown

of about 600 feet in northwestern West Virginia.

WV 7, 5.1 miles west of Kingwood

"ARTHURDALE"

Col. John Fairfax's old plantation. He was aide to Gen. Washington in the Revolution and at one time was superintendent of Mt. Vernon. The mansion was built in 1818. Federal homestead project here was model for others.

WV 92, Arthurdale

ARTHURDALE

Established 1933-34 under Federal Homestead Act, one of several model planned-communities nationwide, and a pet project of Eleanor Roosevelt, to assist unemployed through self-sufficient farming and handicrafts. Town built on 2,400 acres, included 165 homes on 4-acre plots; schools; chicken and dairy farms; furniture, pottery, metal and textile shops; a store, community hall and an inn.

WV 92, 1.4 miles from junction with WV 7, Arthurdale

BIG INJUN SAND

The cross-bedded pebbly formation at the base of Greenbrier Limestone at this site, the "Big Injun Sand" of the driller, is called the Loyalhanna Member. It produces large quantities of oil and natural gas at depths of about 2000 feet in West Virginia.

WV 7, east of Greer

PUTNAM COUNTY

Formed in 1848 from Cabell, Mason, and Kanawha. Named for Gen. Israel Putnam, a Revolutionary War hero. The county is cut by trails made by American bison to the Ohio River. Its oldest town, Buffalo, is named for them.

*US 60, Putnam-Cabell border; WV 34, Putnam-Jackson border; US 35, Putnam-Kanawha border; *WV 25, Putnam-Kanawha border; *US 60, Putnam-Kanawha border; WV 62, Putnam-Kanawha border; WV 34, Putnam-Lincoln border; *US 35, Putnam-Mason border; *WV 62, Putnam-Mason border*

MILITARY SURVEY/NITRO

December 1, 1773, George Washington patented 21,941 acres known as the "Pocatalico Survey." Included were the present sites of Nitro, Sattes, Poca and Cross Lanes. The tract was divided among eight former officers who served in the French and Indian War (1754-1763): Adam Stephen, John Savage, Andrew Lewis, John Wilper, Thomas Bullitt, Peter Hogg, William Wright and John Fry.

Founded Nov. 1, 1917 as site of U.S. Govt. "Explosive Plant C." Thompson Sterratt Co. finished job in eleven months with work force of 110,000. Project included a town to support a population of 24,000 and cost $60 million. Plant operated by Hercules Powder Co. made 350 tons of cannon powder daily. Bought by Charleston Industrial Corp. Nov.

The circa 1877 Hurricane Baptist Church is no longer standing.

1919 and resold to Monsanto, FMC and Fike cos.

US 35, 0.6 miles east of Sattes Bridge, Nitro

BATTLE OF SCARY

First Confederate victory in Kanawha Valley fought here July 17, 1861. Charge of the Rangers under Captain (later General) Jenkins won the day. Whitelaw Reid described the event as a war correspondent with Gen. Cox's Union forces.

US 35, 0.1 miles south of junction with County Route 33 (Teays Valley Road), 2 miles north of St. Albans

HURRICANE BAPTIST CHURCH/ HURRICANE BRIDGE SKIRMISH

Hurricane Baptist Church was founded May 26, 1860, near the old Hurricane Bridge. F.H. Reynolds was first clerk and James Mitchell, the first moderator. This log meeting-house was burned in 1863 by soldiers of the Civil War. Its congregation was scattered but reassembled in 1871. April 2, 1877, it received a deed from C.P. Huntington, president of the Central Land Company, for the site of the present Baptist structure.

Federal troops of the 13th Virginia Volunteer Infantry, commanded by Colonel W.R. Brown, encamped here, were engaged in a five-hour skirmish with a Confederate force commanded by General Albert G. Jenkins, March 28, 1863. Defeated, the Confederates withdrew and continued their march toward their objective, Point Pleasant, where it was rumored that a vast quantity of Federal stores was deposited.

US 60, at junction with WV 34, just south of Hurricane

WASHINGTON'S LAND

This "Poca River Tract" of 7,276 acres was acquired by George Washington, and surveyed by Wm. Crawford, 1773. It bordered Kanawha River, "12 miles and 227 poles". Washington's nephew, Lawrence, resided at Red House Shoals.

*WV 62, in roadside park, 1.2 miles north of Bancroft

ANDREW & CHARLES LEWIS MARCH

The nearby highway is part of route traversing W.Va. from Lewisburg to Point Pleasant memorialized by the state to commemorate the march of the American Colonial army of 1,200 men led by Andrew & Charles Lewis. After a month's march this army defeated a Shawnee Indian force led by Cornstalk at the Battle of Point Pleasant on the banks of the Ohio & Kanawha rivers, October 10, 1774.

WV 62, at roadside park, west of Bancroft

WINFIELD

Named for General Winfield Scott, hero of the Mexican War. In attack upon Federal troops entrenched here in 1864, the Confederates were repulsed and Captain Philip Thurmond killed. The Union rifle pits may still be seen.

US 35, courthouse square, Winfield

RED HOUSE SHOALS/
CIVIL WAR ACTION

Oldest community on the Kanawha River between Charleston and Point Pleasant, being settled circa 1795. In 1819, steamboat "Robert Thompson" failed to navigate the shoals here on a trip to Charleston. This led to an 1820 Act of Virginia Assembly providing for the first improvements on the river. By 1823 cargo boats could travel to Charleston safely. By 1830, tow boats with barges were making the trip.

During the Civil War, there was conflict in this area as armies vied for control of the Kanawha River. Local action included a skirmish here, battles at Scary Creek and Cross Lanes in 1861, and a battle at Winfield in 1864. Armies met twice at Hurricane in 1863 and again in 1864. Union General E.P. Scammon, his boat, and several men were captured at this place 2 February 1864 in a surprise raid by the Confederates.

WV 62, 0.9 miles west of Winfield Bridge (WV 34), Red House

Putnam County Courthouse, Winfield, date unknown

143

RED HOUSE

Site of Federal homestead project, located on land granted to George Washington in 1773. The "Red House" was built by Joseph Ruffner in 1840. Here, February 2, 1864, General E.P. Scammon, Union commander, was captured by Confederates.

WV 62, 1.7 miles west of Winfield Bridge (WV 34), Eleanor

INDIAN VILLAGE/EXCAVATIONS

The Buffalo Indian Village and Cemetery, between the road and the Kanawha River, was one of the largest Indian towns in West Virginia. It was occupied about 1650 by Shawnee Indians who later moved westward.

Excavations, 1963-64, showed a central plaza surrounded by large ceremonial buildings and a semi-circle of ordinary houses; all were enclosed by a stockade. Hundreds of burials were found at this Fort Ancient village site.

WV 62, just east of Buffalo

BUFFALO ACADEMY

Established in 1849 by a joint stock company. First principal was George Rosetter. The school flourished until Civil War began, when it was occupied alternately by soldiers of the Federal and Confederate armies. After the War, the property was deeded to the Buffalo District Board of Education. One of the students at Buffalo during the academy years, John McCausland, became an illustrious Confederate General.

WV 62, Buffalo

"LAWNVALE"/"COIN" HARVEY

One mile north, home of Dr. T.C. Atkeson, head of Grange for many years. Dean of the W.Va. College of Agriculture and author of many works on agriculture. For nearly 50 years, Atkeson was a leader among farmers of America.

Birthplace of William Hope "Coin" Harvey, son of Colonel Robert Harvey. Builder of a pyramid at Monte Ne, Ark. Author of "Coin's Financial School" in 1894 and other works on finance, which proposed silver inflation.

WV 62, Buffalo

RALEIGH COUNTY

Formed, 1850, from Fayette. Named for Sir Walter Raleigh, who planted the first English colony in America. Beckley, the county seat, was founded by Alfred Beckley, and named for his father, John, first clerk of the House of Representatives.

*WV 3, Raleigh-Boone border; WV 41, Raleigh-Fayette border; *WV 61, Raleigh-Fayette border; *US 19/WV 16, Raleigh-Fayette border; *US 19, Raleigh-Mercer border; WV 3, Raleigh-Summers border; *WV 54, Raleigh-Wyoming border; WV 16, Raleigh-Wyoming border; *WV 99, Raleigh-Wyoming border*

BECKLEY

Created Apr. 4, 1838. Named for John Beckley, clerk of the House of Representatives in terms of Washington, Adams, and Jefferson. General Alfred Beckley, his son, had home, "Park Place", later known as "Wildwood", built here in 1835.

Main Street, courthouse square, Beckley

ECCLES MINE EXPLOSIONS

Five miles west at Eccles, on April 28, 1914, a gas explosion in No. 5 Mine in the Beckley seam killed 174 miners; another nine died in No. 6 Mine above from blackdamp. On March 8, 1926, 19 died in No. 5. In 1891, Royal Mine on New River was first to open in Raleigh County. From 1891 to 1991, county mines produced in excess of 791M tons of coal, while accidents claimed the lives of 2,121 miners.

Main Street, courthouse square, Beckley

WILDWOOD

Built by John Lilly, Sr. in 1835-36, it was the home of Alfred Beckley (1802-88) and Amelia Neville Craig. Son of John Beckley, first clerk of the House of Representatives, he founded the town of Beckley and wrote the bill proposing formation of Raleigh County. An 1823 West Point graduate, he rose to rank of Brig. Gen. in the Civil War. Listed on National Register in 1971, and opened as a House Museum in 1986.

Off Laurel Terrace, behind 1400 block of South Kanawha Street, Beckley

PINECREST SANITARIUM

Established in 1927 by act of the Legislature to provide additional facilities for sufferers from tuberculosis. Opened to the public, 1930. Capacity increased, 1938. Early treatment of the disease is emphasized. Altitude 2350 feet.

Wildwood, built 1835-36, was the home of Alfred Beckley, founder of Beckley. The house is now owned by the Raleigh County Historical Society.

US 19, at junction with Bailey Avenue, Beckley

VETERANS ADMINISTRATION HOSPITAL

Erected, 1948-1950. Opened for patients March 1, 1951. A one hundred seventy-two bed General Medical and Surgical Service Hospital and a forty-two bed Nursing Home Care Unit, dedicated to the medical care of eligible veterans.

Off US 19, at entrance to hospital, Beckley

RALEIGH COUNTY COAL MINES

The county's first mine opened at Royal on the New River in 1891. The Beckley Exhibition Mine, once an actual operating mine, and the dozens of others throughout Ra-

leigh County produced 792,055,155 tons of bituminous coal in the first century of the county's coal industry, 1891-1991. Employment at the county mines ran as high as 14,226 annually.

Off US 19, near Beckley Exhibition Coal Mine, Beckley

GRANDVIEW PARK

Grandview Park (11 miles N.) 878 acres, derives name from an overhanging cliff 1300 feet high. In basal Pennsylvania rocks. New River in this area has cut a steep-walled gorge through Mauch Chunk strata of late Mississippian Age.

*US 19/WV 3, Daniels

Visitors to the Beckley Exhibition Coal Mine get an up-close look at Raleigh County's mining tradition.

Part of the New River Gorge National River, Grandview is known for its spectacular views of the New River.

HUFF'S KNOB

To the west is Huff's Knob. This peak, nearly 3800 feet high, is the summit of the Flat Top Mountain range. The view from its top commands a complete circle of the most beautiful regions of Raleigh, Mercer, and Summers counties.

*US 19, Raleigh-Mercer border

SITE OF MARK TWAIN HIGH SCHOOL

From 1921-65 school served students from coal towns Hot Coal, Big Stick, Woodbay, McAlpin, Stotesbury, Tams, Ury, Helen, Amigo, Sophia and Slab Fork. Robert C. Byrd, valedictorian, Mark Twain High School class of 1934, served in WV Leg. (1947-53) & Con-

gress (1953-59). Elected to Senate in 1958, Senator Byrd held every major leadership position, was third in line for presidency and noted Senate scholar.

County Route 30, Stotesbury

RANDOLPH COUNTY

Formed from Harrison in 1787. Named for Edmund Jennings Randolph, Virginia statesman and soldier. Largest county in the State. Federal dominance of the Tygarts Valley in War between the States largely determined control of W.Va.

US 250, Randolph-Barbour border; US 33, Randolph-Pendleton border; US 219,

147

*Randolph-Pocahontas border; US 250, Randolph-Pocahontas border; US 219, Randolph-Tucker border; *WV 32, Randolph-Tucker border; *US 33, Randolph-Upshur border; WV 15, Randolph-Webster border*

FOSSIL TREE PARK

Millions of years ago much of West Virginia was a sea bed. Here is found evidence of this in the large number of fossilized trees, among which are examples 10 feet in diameter. This formation is more than 50 miles long.

US 33, 0.1 miles west of junction with County Route 11 (Laurel Mountain Road), just west of Elkins

W.VA. CHILDREN'S HOME

Established in 1909 to give a home for orphans and for neglected children. Children are kept here until 18 years old unless a home has been found for them. Educational advantages and home training are offered.

US 219, 0.2 miles north of junction with US 33, Elkins

ELKINS

Named for Senator Stephen B. Elkins. Home of Senator Henry G. Davis. Headquarters for the Monongahela National Forest. Near site of Friend's Fort, built 1772. Old Seneca Indian Trail crosses the campus of Davis and Elkins College.

Randolph and High streets, courthouse square, Elkins

HALLIEHURST/ STEPHEN BENTON ELKINS

Summer home of Sen. Stephen B. Elkins. Named for his wife, Hallie Davis Elkins. Built 1889-1891, at cost of $300,000. Largest shingle-style home in WV. Deeded to Davis & Elkins College, 1923. National Historic Landmark, 1988.

Businessman, politician, co-founder City of Elkins. Born in Ohio, 1841; died in Washington, DC, 1911. Secretary of War, 1891-1893; U.S. Senator from WV, 1895-1911. National figure in Republican Party for more than 30 years.

US 33, at junction with US 219, Elkins

KUMP HOUSE/HERMAN GUY KUMP

Home of Gov. Herman Guy Kump. Built 1924-25, on site of Civil War-era Goddin Tavern. Designed by Clarence Harding of Washington, DC. Eleanor Roosevelt and other notables were guests during 1930s and '40s. Named to National Register in 1983.

Herman Guy Kump
19th governor of West Virginia

Born in Hampshire Co., 1877; died 1962, in Elkins. As 19th Governor of WV, he led state out of Depression. State Road, Parks & Forest, County Unit School systems, and Dept. of Public Assistance all date from his administration, 1933-37.

US 33, at junction with US 219, Elkins

BIG LIME AND BIG INJUN SANDS

The Greenbrier Limestone in the quarry represents the "Big Lime" and "Big Injun Sand" of the driller. Fish-egg like oölitic zones in the "Big Lime" and the basal sandy formation, the "Big Injun", yield oil and natural gas in West Virginia.

Old US 33 (County Route 33/8), approximately 0.5 miles from junction with US 33, east of Elkins

SENECA TRAIL/TORY CAMPS

The Seneca Trail passed near here from the Tygart Valley to the South Branch Valley. Thousands of horses and cattle captured by Generals Imboden and Jones in 1863 crossed the mountains by this trail.

Near Harman can still be seen remains of two Tory camps where some British sympathizers hid during the American Revolution. They encamped here, 1775-1776, to escape laws enacted against them by Virginia.

US 33/WV 55, 2.8 miles west of Harman

BIG LIME AND BIG INJUN

The Greenbrier Limestone in the quarry represents the "Big Lime

and "Big Injun Sand" of the driller. Fish-egg like (oölitic) zones in the "Big Lime" and the basal sandy formation, the "Big Injun", produce oil and natural gas in West Virginia.

WV 32, 0.3 miles north of Harman

BENJAMIN WILSON

In 1774 Capt. Benjamin Wilson was made a colonel in Lord Dunmore's army when it invaded the Indian country. He was active in concluding peace with western Indians at the Pickaway Plains in Ohio after the Battle of Point Pleasant.

US 219/US 250, at junction with Ward Road (County Route 23), just north of Midland

WILSON'S FORT

Here, 1772, settled Captain Benjamin Wilson, commanding Wilson, Friend, Roney forts. Had built, 1774, Currence, Westfall, Haddan forts. Fort Wilson was important military post. The first county court met here.

*US 219/US 250, 5 miles south of Elkins

BEVERLY COVERED BRIDGE

Site of old covered bridge on Staunton & Parkersburg Turnpike built in 1847 by Lemuel Chenoweth (1811-87). Burned during Civil War, he rebuilt it in 1873. Dismantled by state in 1951. Chenoweth's home, built in 1847, is southeast of old bridge site.

Junction of Water and Bridge Streets, one block west of US 219, Beverly

The battle of Rich Mountain was waged around the Hart House, near Beverly. The house was destroyed by fire in 1940. Date unknown.

RICH MOUNTAIN/
CROZET-CHENOWETH

At Rich Mountain, 5 miles west, July 11, 1861, Federal forces defeated Confederate troops whose trenches may still be seen. Military reputations of Gen. Geo. B. McClellan and of Gen. W.S. Rosecrans were established by this victory.

Memorial road to Col. Claudius Crozet, leader in building the Northwestern and the Staunton and Parkersburg turnpikes. Here was the home of Lemuel Chenoweth, who designed and built many wooden bridges in W.Va. which became famous.

US 219, Beverly

BEVERLY

Settled about 1753 by Robert Files and David Tygart. Files' family was massacred near by. Site of Westfall's Fort, 1774. In Mt. Iser Cemetery are the Union trenches and graves of Confederate soldiers killed in Battle of Rich Mountain.

US 219, Beverly

LEMUEL CHENOWETH

Local carpenter, legislator, officeholder, self-educated architect and the state's most famous builder and designer of covered bridges, Lemuel Chenoweth lived in Randolph County his entire life, 1811-1887. Bridges at Barrackville & Philippi are two major examples of his work. Several homes and Huttonsville

Presbyterian Church are among his other credits. He is buried in Beverly Cemetery.

US 219, Beverly

RICH MOUNTAIN/HART HOUSE

Battle of Rich Mountain fought here July 11, 1861. In a surprise attack, Gen. W.S. Rosecrans defeated Confederates led by Capt. J.A. deLagnel. Battle was decisive in McClellan's N.W. Virginia campaign.

Rich Mountain battle was waged near Hart House and barn where deLagnel's 310 men held Rosecrans' forces for 4 hours before surrendering. This forced Col. Pegram to retreat. His army was captured.

County Route 37/8 (Rich Mountain Road), 5.2 miles west of Beverly

U.S. HOMESTEAD

Here the United States Government was maintaining one of three homestead projects operating in West Virginia. The old Hornbeck Cemetery and the site of the cabin of David Tygart, pioneer settler, are in this vicinity.

US 219, at junction with County Route 21 (East Dailey Road), Dailey

HELVETIA

Settled by a group of Swiss and German immigrants who came via Brooklyn, NY in 1869. In addition to farmers and herdsmen, many craftsmen and professionals were among the settlers: stone masons, carpenters and painters; wagon, shoe, watch, hat and cheese mak-

Randolph County town of Helvetia, date unknown

151

ers; musicians, teachers, ministers and doctors. Later groups from Switzerland and other parts of the U.S. boosted 1875 population to 308.

County Route 46 (Mill Creek Road), at junction with County Route 45 (Pickens Road), Helvetia; County Route 46 (Mill Creek Road), 0.2 miles from junction with County Route 45 (Pickens Road), Helvetia

ARMY HEADQUARTERS, 1861/ HUTTONSVILLE

This village was held by Colonel George Porterfield until he was relieved of command by General Robert Garnett (C.S.A.). In 1861, it became the headquarters of Generals George McClellan and J.J. Reynolds of the Union Army.

Named for Jonathan Hutton, its first postmaster, in 1813. Students from the local academy joined the Confederate Army, 1861. The first military telegraph to advance with an army in America came here, July, 1861.

US 219, 0.1 miles from junction with US 250, Huttonsville

BISHOP ASBURY

Bishop Francis Asbury, famed Methodist circuit rider, often visited the Potomac, Tygart's, Greenbrier and Monongahela Valleys. In 1790, on a journey from Georgia to New England, he preached at cabin of Benjamin Wilson in Tygart's Valley.

US 219/US 250, 0.4 miles north of junction, Huttonsville

Bishop Francis Asbury (1745-1816)

ELKWATER/COL. J.A. WASHINGTON

Trenches made by Federal troops under Gen. Reynolds, 1861. Nearby were the two Haddan Indian forts, scene of the Stewart and Kinnan massacres. Important features of 4-H Club work among rural youth started here in 1915.

Here, Sept. 13, 1861, Col. John Augustine Washington, aide-de-camp to Gen. Robert E. Lee, C.S.A., was killed. He was the last of resident owners of Mt. Vernon, which he had sold in 1859 to become a national shrine.

US 219, 0.5 miles from junction with Kumbrabow Road, Elkwater

THE CONLEY GRAVES

Nearby is the burial place of Darby Conley (Connolly) and members of his family, victims of an Indian attack on this upper Tygart Valley settlement in 1777 ("bloody year of the three sevens"). One headstone marks graves.

US 219, 4.8 miles from junction with Kumbrabow Road, near Elkwater

INDIAN MOUND

The Hyre-Crouch Mound, on the terrace above highway, was totally excavated and reconstructed by the State, 1963. Twenty burials were found, chiefly "bundle", and one cremation in a pit at the base of the mound, built by the Armstrong Culture between A.D. 1-500. Scattered camp site remains were also found on the terrace. Projectile points, pottery and a copper bead were found in the mound, situated on the Randolph Crouch property.

US 219, 4 miles south of Elkwater

BIG LIME

The Greenbrier Limestone in this quarry is the "Big Lime" of the driller. Fish-egg like (oölitic) zones in the "Big Lime" yield oil and natural gas in West Virginia.

*WV 15, east of Monterville

VALLEY HEAD

In 1777, Indians killed Darby Connolly and several members of his family on Connolly Run. Other settlers were taken captive. At Indian Run in 1780, three members of surveying party under Jacob Warwick were killed by the Indians.

US 219, 0.5 miles south of junction with WV 15, Valley Head

MINGO FLATS

Named for the Mingo Indians who had a village here. This tribe was a branch of the Iroquois. The Seneca Indian Trail passes this point. On Valley Mountain in 1861, Gen. Rob-

ert E. Lee camped while campaigning in this valley.

US 219, Mingo

LEE'S HEADQUARTERS

One-half mile east is the site of Gen. R.E. Lee's Valley Mountain Headquarters where he camped with his troops from Aug. 6 to Sept. 20, 1861 while he directed the ill-fated Cheat Mountain Campaign.

US 219, 0.5 miles north of Randolph-Pocahontas border

OLD BRICK CHURCH

Tygart's Valley Presbyterian Church, organized in 1820. A brick building erected three-fourths mile west at the cemetery was destroyed by Union soldiers in 1862-1863 and the bricks used for building flues at the winter quarters.

US 250, 1.1 miles south of junction with US 219, Huttonsville

FORT MILROY

Fortified camp of Federal troops on White Top Mountain above the 4000-foot level, was highest military camp in War Between the States. Its command of the Staunton and Parkersburg Turnpike blocked General Lee's army.

*US 250, south of Huttonsville

ASA GRAY/BUFFALO INDIAN TRAIL

Asa Gray, famous Harvard botanist, discovered plants new to science as he crossed Cheat Mountain by way of Staunton-Parkersburg Turnpike,

August, 1843. He was one of original 50 named to New York Hall of Fame.

Remnants of a Buffalo-Indian Trail as well as a wagon road of a 1788 survey can still be seen near the place where the Staunton-Parkersburg Turnpike crossed Cheat Mountain Summit, one-fourth mile west.

US 250, near junction with County Route 250/4, near Randolph-Pocahontas border

CHEAT SUMMIT CAMP

Also called Fort Milroy. Fortified camp in gap at the crest of White Top of Cheat Mountain. Occupied by Federal troops during fall and winter of 1861-1862; repulsed threats in Lee's mountain campaign of 1861. Fort's command of the Parkersburg-Staunton Turnpike prevented Lee's army from advancing inland. Above 4,000 feet elevation, highest Union fort in the Civil War.

US 250, at junction with County Route 250/4, near Randolph-Pocahontas border

RITCHIE COUNTY

Formed in 1843 from Lewis, Harrison, and Wood. Named for Thomas Ritchie, Virginia journalist. In 1772, Elias and Jesse Hughes and Colonel William Lowther explored this region to the Ohio. Hughes River was named by them.

*WV 16, Ritchie-Calhoun border; County Route 50/30 (Old US 50), Ritchie-Doddridge border; *WV 47, Ritchie-Gilmer*

*border; WV 16, Ritchie-Pleasants border; *WV 74, Ritchie-Tyler border; *WV 47, Ritchie-Wirt border; *WV 53, Ritchie-Wirt border; *US 50, Ritchie-Wood border*

TOLLGATE

The Northwestern Turnpike, a favorite project of George Washington, opened in 1838. Such highways were called "turnpikes" from the gates at which tolls were collected. This town is named for the toll gate which stood here.

County Route 10, near junction with US 50, Toll Gate

PENNSBORO

Settled by John Bunnell, a veteran of the Revolution, near the salt lick which attracted great game herds. The "Stone House", built about 1807 by John Webster, was one of the famous inns on the Northwestern Turnpike.

WV 74, Myles Stadium, Pennsboro

THE STONE HOUSE

The Webster House, now known as The Stone House, was built shortly after 1800. The walls of the house are two feet thick, constructed of flagstones of various shapes and sizes held together by cement and mortar. John Webster, the builder, sold it to James Martin in 1815. It remained in the Martin family until 1908 when it was sold to A.J. Ireland. In 1820, the first post office in Ritchie County was located in The Stone House and James Martin became the county's first postmaster. For

Parade in Harrisville, circa 1890s

many years the only house between Clarksburg and the Parkersburg-Marietta area, it served as a stage-coach inn. Horses were kept there for exchange on the trip.

WV 74, Pennsboro

HARRISVILLE

Named for Thomas Harris. His nephew, General Thomas Harris, distinguished himself in the Union Army at Petersburg and Cedar Creek. He was one of the commissioners who tried those charged with plotting assassination of Lincoln.

WV 16 and WV 31, Harrisville

General Thomas Harris

INDIAN BATTLES

In this vicinity in 1769, Jesse Hughes and party routed a band of Indians. To the north on Indian Creek in 1781, Colonel William Lowther led a party which killed five Indians and rescued Tygarts Valley white captives.

*WV 47, Macfarlan

ROANE COUNTY

Formed in 1856 from Gilmer, Jackson and Kanawha. Named for Judge Spencer Roane of Virginia. Land grants in 1787 and 1795 to Albert Gallatin and friends and to Samuel Hopkins and the Tiersons included most of the county.

*US 33, Roane-Calhoun border; *WV 36, Roane-Clay border; US 33, Roane-Jackson border; *US 119, Roane-Kanawha border; *WV 14, Roane-Wirt border

View of Spencer showing the former state hospital in the foreground. The hospital buildings are no longer standing. Date unknown.

SPENCER

Visited, 1771, by James Hughes, Indian fighter and scout. In 1812, named Tanner's Cross Roads for Samuel Tanner. To the west on the Marcellus Hart farm is the deepest oil or gas well east of the Mississippi River, 9104 feet.

US 33, courthouse square, Spencer

SPENCER STATE HOSPITAL

Second of the four hospitals provided by the State of West Virginia to care for the mentally ill. This institution was authorized in 1887 and was completed in 1893.

*US 33, Spencer

POCATALICO RIVER

The Pocatalico River keeps alive the Indian word which meant "Plenty of Fat Doe". Here early hunters and trappers brought their furs and by canoe made their way down this stream to Great Kanawha River and markets.

US 119, 0.1 miles south of County Route 34, Walton

SUMMERS COUNTY

Formed, 1871, from Monroe, Fayette, Greenbrier, Mercer. Named for the distinguished jurist of Kanawha, George W. Summers. Dr. Thomas Walker and companions explored the Greenbrier Valley, 1750, for the Greenbrier Company.

WV 20, Summers-Fayette border; *WV 3, Summers-Greenbrier border; WV 20, Summers-Mercer border; WV 12, Summers-Monroe border; WV 3, Summers-Raleigh border

STATE PRISON FOR WOMEN

Established, 1947, by an act of the legislature as a state prison for women. A program of rehabilitation is provided in vocational and crafts training. This property was the famous Pence Springs Resort Hotel of the early 1900s.

*WV 3, Pence Springs

FORT GREENBRIER
Near site of Fort Greenbrier, commanded by Capt. John Van Bibber during Indian raids in 1777. Here stands house built, 1772, by Col. James Graham, with walls pierced for rifle fire. Graham's son was killed and daughter captured by Indians.

WV 3/WV 12, between Pence Springs and Talcott

BIG BEND TUNNEL
The great tunnel of the C&O Railroad was started at Big Bend in 1870 and completed three years later. It is more than a mile long, and now has a twin tunnel. Tradition makes this the scene of the steel drivers' ballad, "John Henry."

WV 3/WV 12, just west of Talcott

Statue of John Henry near Big Bend Tunnel, site of the epic struggle between man and machine.

WRECK ON THE C&O
Across Greenbrier River, on October 23, 1890, engineer George Washington Alley (b. July 10, 1860) was scalded to death. Engine #134, pulling Fast Flying Virginian from Cincinnati to Washington, hit a boulder on tracks. Lewis Withrow & Robert Foster, firemen, injured. Alley, pinned in cab, died before rescuers & family could free him. Solemnized in verse & song "The Wreck on the C&O" & "Fatal Run."

WV 3, 0.8 miles from junction with WV 20/WV 3, Bellepoint

FORT CULBERTSON
South on New River at Crump's Bottom, Fort Culbertson was built, 1774, at outbreak of Dunmore's War by Capt. James Robertson on order of William Preston, Lieutenant-Colonel of Fincastle County. This fort was garrisoned by troops.

WV 3 (Greenbrier Drive), at junction with Cedar Avenue, Hinton

HINTON
Named for its founder. Indian raids broke up early settlements in southern part of this county. First permanent settlements were those of James Graham at Lowell and of Robert Lilly on Little Bluestone from 1770 to 1772.

WV 3, courthouse square, Hinton

HOME OF JACK WARHOP
Babe Ruth's first two major league home runs, 6 May and 2 June 1915, were hit off pitcher, John Wauhop,

1884-1960, at the Polo Grounds in NY. Wauhop, playing under name of Warhop and "Chief," played for Highlanders, who became the NY Yankees, Sept. 1908-15, compiling record of 69 wins and 93 losses for .426 avg. Born on Powley's Ck., he played for Hinton C&O RR team.

Belle Point Park, Hinton

ANDREW & CHARLES LEWIS MARCH

The nearby highway is part of route to Point Pleasant memorialized by the state to commemorate the march of the American Colonial army of 1,200 men led by Andrew & Charles Lewis. After a month's march this army defeated a Shawnee Indian force led by Cornstalk at the Battle of Point Pleasant on the banks of the Ohio & Kanawha rivers, October 10, 1774.

WV 20, Green Sulphur Springs

GILES, FAYETTE & KANAWHA TURNPIKE

Approx. site of 40 mile post of 118 mile turnpike auth. 1838 by Va. leg. Cap: $42,600, ($16,000 state). Cost: $25,429. Route: Pearisburg, Giles Co. to Peterstown & Red Sulphur; crossed New at Indian Creek to Bluestone and forded near here; along Bluestone Mt. to John's Knob & Jumping Br.; across White Oak Mt. to Glade Creek; to Mt. Hope, Fayetteville, Cotton Hill and Kanawha R. Old Farley Trace nearby.

*County Route 20/2, at junction with

County Route 3/45, Bluestone State Park, near Hinton

PIPESTEM FALLS

Name derived from the hollow stemmed shrub Spiraea alba which grows profusely along Big and Little Pipestem creeks. The first white man to see Pipestem was Christopher Gist, 1750, while exploring for the Ohio Land Company. Shawnee Indians camped near this site in 1774. They used the hollow stemmed shrub, as later did the white settlers, for pipestems. A beautiful, fully equipped State Park is located at the site.

*WV 20, north of Pipestem

JORDAN'S CHAPEL

1st frame church in the area, located .8 mi. NW. Built 1852 in the Greek Revival style. Prominent local brothers Gordon & Thomas Jordan gave land and lumber. Used by the Methodists many years.

WV 20, at junction with County Route 18 (True Road), north of Pipestem

MERCER SALT WORKS

The Mercer Salt Works at the junction of New River and Lick Creek supplied salt to southern West Virginia until destroyed, Aug. 10, 1862, by the cavalry of Col. Rutherford B. Hayes, 23d Ohio Regiment, encamped at Green Meadows.

WV 20, at junction with County Route 26 (Lick Creek Road), 0.2 miles north of Pipestem

"NEELY PLANTATION"

John "Buttermilk" W. Neely, Sr. (1780-1865) & Delilah Sweeney Neely (1784-1851) settled here in 1822 on 3,000 acres and reared 10 children. Property comprised total area of Pipestem St. Park. Nearby, Pipestem Knob is site of former Neely home and burial grounds. Pipestem Knob Primitive Baptist log church at east base, on former Indian trail, was active until relocated for construction of Pipestem State Park.

WV 20, 0.1 miles south of Pipestem State Park

TAYLOR COUNTY

Formed, 1844, from Marion, Harrison and Barbour. Named for John Taylor of Virginia. This county was the home of Bailey Brown, first Union soldier killed in the Civil War. He was shot, May 22, 1861, at Fetterman, now Grafton.

*US 119 and US 250, Taylor-Barbour border; WV 76, Taylor-Barbour border; *County Route 73, Taylor-Harrison border; WV 76, Taylor-Harrison border; *US 50, Taylor-Harrison border; Old County Route 73, Taylor-Marion border; *US 250, Taylor-Marion border; *WV 310, Taylor-Marion border; US 119, Taylor-Monongalia border; US 50, Taylor-Preston border*

WEST VIRGINIA COLLEGE

Opened on this site in 1865 by Free Will Baptists led by local resident Rev. F.J. Cather. Chartered by the legislature June 26, 1868. Rev. A.D. Williams became first president and

West Virginia College, Flemington, date unknown

159

served until 1870 when he resigned to become Supt. of Free Schools in W.Va. It functioned into the 1890's when reduced enrollments forced its closing. Building served Flemington High School until razed in 1950's.

County Route 13, 0.8 miles east of junction with WV 76, Flemington

FLEMINGTON
Named for early settlers. Here Colonel Johnson C. Fleming about 1867 made demonstration of the "glider". Near here lived Thomas Allen, the messenger of Wellington at Waterloo. He died here at the age of 107. (4 Mi. South.)

WV 76, Flemington

JOHN SIMPSON
Here John Simpson, hunter and trapper, stopped in 1763. He moved on to Clarksburg in 1764. Harrison and Taylor Counties keep alive his memory in the names of Simpson Creek, the town of Simpson and Simpson District.

County Route 13, Simpson

ANNA JARVIS' BIRTHPLACE
Anna Jarvis was born here, 5-1-1864. Through her efforts President Wilson designated in 1914 the second Sunday in May as Mother's Day. She died 11-24-1948 and was buried in West Laurel Hill Cemetery, Bala-Cynwyd, Pennsylvania.

US 119/US 250, Webster

VALLEY FALLS
Beauty spot six miles north of the boundary of Taylor and Marion counties where Tygarts Valley River dashes through a mile-long gorge in series of lovely falls and rapids. Included in 1000-acre grant to Thomas Parkeson in 1773.

US 50, at junction with WV 310, Pruntytown

Anna Maria Reeves Jarvis (1832-1905), left, and her daughter Anna (1864-1948), the founder of Mother's Day

Aerial view of Grafton with Tygart Dam shown in the background, date unknown

PRUNTYTOWN

Settled by John and David Prunty about 1798. It was county seat, 1844 to 1878. Site of old Rector College. Birthplace of John Barton Payne, Secretary of Interior under Wilson, and head of the American Red Cross.

*US 50, Pruntytown

INDUSTRIAL SCHOOL FOR BOYS

The West Virginia Industrial School for Boys was established in 1889 by an act of the Legislature and was formally opened July 21, 1891 for the purpose of training boys committed to the Institution by the courts of West Virginia.

US 250, 0.1 miles south of junction with US 50, Pruntytown

JOHN BARTON PAYNE

To north stood birthplace of John Barton Payne (1855-1935), Secretary of the Interior in cabinet of President Woodrow Wilson. From 1921 until his death in 1935, he was chairman of the American Red Cross.

*US 50, Pruntytown

GRAFTON

William Robinson preempted Buffalo Flats, site of Grafton, in 1773. Here is only National cemetery in State. Former home of John T. McGraw, financier, and Melville

Davisson Post, author. Anna Jarvis, founder of Mother's Day, lived here.

US 119, at junction with US 50, Grafton

FEDERAL DAM
Great dam built by United States Government two miles south on the Tygarts Valley River to control floods in the Monongahela Valley. It is 210 feet high and 1780 feet long. It forms a lake of over 4000 acres, 73 miles around.

US 50/US 119, Grafton

OLD CATHOLIC CEMETERY
About 500 graves of early Grafton settlers, dating 1857-1917, are in old cemetery located on land given by Sarah Fetterman to St. Augustine Catholic Church. Headstones include names of Irish and German emigrants. Buried here is Thomas McGraw, B&O Railroad construction supervisor, local merchant and father of John T.—lawyer, banker, politician, and coal, railroad and lumber developer.

US 50, at junction with Market Street, Grafton

NATIONAL CEMETERY
The first National Military Cemetery in West Virginia is located on Walnut Street in Grafton. Established in 1867 for permanent burial of Civil

Grafton National Cemetery contains more than 2,100 burials and includes the graves of soldiers from the Civil War to present.

The current Fairfax Stone Monument is the fifth such monument erected near the head spring of the North Branch of the Potomac River.

War dead. Bailey Brown, the first Union soldier killed in the War, is buried here.

Walnut Street and Armstrong Avenue, off US 119, Grafton

ANNA JARVIS

In St. Andrews Methodist Church, Main Street, Grafton, the first official Mother's Day service was held on May 10, 1908, through efforts of Anna Jarvis. President Wilson in 1914 set aside the second Sunday in May as Mother's Day.

*US 50, near State Police Barracks, Grafton

TUCKER COUNTY

Formed, 1856, from Randolph. Named for Henry St. George Tucker, eminent jurist and statesman of Virginia. In this county is a part of the vast Monongahela National Forest. Blackwater Falls and Canaan Valley are also features.

WV 38, Tucker-Barbour border; *WV 90, Tucker-Grant border; *US 219, Tucker-Preston border; WV 72, Tucker-Preston border; *WV 32, Tucker-Randolph border; US 219, Tucker-Randolph border

FAIRFAX STONE

The Fairfax Stone (1/2 Mi. E.), marking the Potomac's headwaters, was a corner of Lord Fairfax's vast estate. The line of 1736 was checked in 1746 by a survey on which Peter Jefferson, father of Thomas Jefferson, was engaged.

US 219, 1 mile north of junction with WV 90

THE BLACKWATER

To the southeast is Blackwater Falls, 63 feet high, and its rugged gorge. It drains lovely Canaan Valley, which may be seen from the mountain top, 3700 feet high. It was made famous in "Blackwater Chronicles" by "Porte Crayon."

*US 219 and WV 32, Thomas

SALT SANDS

The resistant Homewood and Conoquenessing sandstones, the "Salt Sands" of the driller, form the canyon walls and Blackwater Falls. These sands produce oil and natural gas in West Virginia and commercial brines on the Kanawha and Ohio Rivers.

WV 32, Blackwater Falls State Park, on path to falls; *WV 32, Blackwater Falls State Park, near lodge

SALT SANDS

The massive Pottsville Sandstones exposed here are the same as those in the Blackwater Gorge, and are the "Salt Sands" of the driller. The "Salt Sands" produce oil and natural gas in West Virginia and commercial brines on the Kanawha and Ohio Rivers.

*WV 32, near Canaan Valley State Park

ST. GEORGE

First county seat. Here John Minear and son, Jonathan, after early visits, settled in 1776. Both of them were killed by Indians, 1780-1781. Captain James Parsons and brother, Thomas,

Armed men moved county records from St. George to Parsons in 1893 during the "County Seat War."

made settlements in the Horseshoe, 1772-1774.

WV 72, near St. George

FORT MINEAR/FIRST COUNTY SEAT

Erected by John Minear in 1776, who with a group of immigrants later founded St. George. Settlement site of American Indian raids in spring of 1780. Minear and son Jonathan among those killed in 1781 attack.

Here stood Tucker's first courthouse. Confederate flag raised over it, May 1861. The town changed sides ten times during the Civil War. "County Seat War" ended Aug. 1, 1893, when records removed by armed men.

Main Street, St. George

SAINT GEORGE ACADEMY

Incorporated July 20, 1885 by William H. Lipscomb, John J. Adams, Bascom B. Baker, Ezekiel Harper, Sansome E. Parsons, Wilson B. Maxwell, Adam C. Minear, and William E. Talbott. The school ceased to operate in June, 1893.

County Route 1 (Holly Meadows Road), off County Route 5 (Location Road), 0.5 miles east of WV 72, St. George

Scenic Blackwater Falls near Thomas in Tucker County

PARSONS/CORRICK'S FORD

John Crouch, pioneer settler, established "tomahawk rights" here in 1766, but the town was not incorporated until 1893. Here Shavers Fork and Blackwater unite to form the Cheat River. Hu Maxwell, the historian, lived near.

After the battles of Philippi, Laurel Hill, and Rich Mountain, Gen. R.S. Garnett, new commander of the Confederates, led his army southward through the Tygarts Valley. His force was overtaken at Corrick's Ford, July 13, 1861, defeated, and Garnett killed.

US 219, at junction with WV 72, Parsons

CORRICK'S FORD

After the Confederate defeat in the Tygarts Valley early in 1861, Gen. R.S. Garnett, the Southern leader, withdrew. Here he was overtaken by Federals under his West Point classmate, Gen. T.A. Morris, his army defeated, and himself mortally wounded.

US 219, south side of Parsons

SENECA TRAIL

The Seneca Trail, or Warrior's Path, was the Indian highway from New York to the South. In West Virginia, it followed in general the Alleghenies and this trail, made by moccasined feet centuries ago, may be seen at many points today.

US 219, just north of Randolph-Tucker border

TYLER COUNTY

Formed in 1814 from Ohio. Named for John Tyler, governor of Virginia and father of President Tyler. Here in 1894 was drilled "Big Moses", the greatest gas well in the world, producing one hundred million cubic feet per day.

*WV 18, Tyler-Doddridge border; *WV 23, Tyler-Doddridge border; *WV 2, Tyler-Pleasants border; *WV 74, Tyler-Ritchie border; *WV 2, Tyler-Wetzel border; WV Alternate 18, Tyler-Wetzel border*

ANCIENT RUINS

The prehistoric stone and earth ruins at Ben's Run are among the most extensive to be found in the United States. Two parallel circular walls, several miles in length, and 120 feet apart, enclose an area of more than 400 acres.

WV 2, Ben's Run

SISTERSVILLE

Charles Wells settled here in 1776 and the first county court was held at his home. The town was named in 1815 for the Wells sisters and was incorporated in 1839. A ferry across the Ohio was established here in 1818.

WV 2, at corner of Elizabeth and Wells streets, Sistersville

POLECAT OIL WELL/ "BIG MOSES" WELL

Drilled on Joshua Russell farm 2 mi. North on Polecat Run. Almost abandoned because of presence of salt water, the well was made pro-

Oil wells dot this view of Sistersville, circa 1900

ducer by Ludwig and Weeter's introduction of technology to siphon off water. Drilled to Big Injun sand, it proved the Sistersville anticline, led to Sistersville's boom and to recognition of field as greatest producing area at the turn of the century.

Drilled on Moses Spencer farm on Indian Creek 22 mi. east of Sistersville and attributed greatest in W.Va. Brought in on 6 Sept. 1894, with estimated daily capacity of 100 million cu. ft., Big Moses blew until 28 Nov. Controlled for 3 months, pressure burst casing and well blew until 27 Aug. 1895. Twice fired, reductions in pressure by waste and excessive drilling, led to abandonment.

Riverside Drive, Sistersville

MIDDLEBOURNE

Established, 1813. Named because it was halfway between Pennsylvania and the old salt wells on the Kanawha above Charleston. The "Jug Handle" on Middle Island Creek is one of the noted beauty spots of the Ohio Valley.

Court and Main streets, courthouse square, Middlebourne

UPSHUR COUNTY

Formed in 1851 from Lewis, Barbour and Randolph. Named for Abel Parker Upshur, the great Virginia statesman. Samuel and John Pringle, the first settlers, came in 1764. The Pringle brothers later guided other pioneers here.

*WV 20, Upshur-Barbour border; *US 119, Upshur-Barbour border; *US 33, Upshur-Lewis border; *WV 4, Upshur-Lewis border; *US 33, Upshur-Randolph border; WV 20, Upshur-Webster border*

POPULATION CENTER

The population center of the United States was in present West Virginia four times as it moved westward across the nation: near Wardensville in 1820; at Smoke Hole in 1830; west of Buckhannon in 1840; near Burning Springs in 1850.

US 119/US 33, at junction with County Route 5/1 (Sauls Run Road), Lorentz

LORENTZ

Near here 18 members of the Schoolcraft and Bozarth families were killed or taken prisoner by savages during the Indian wars. Here were the first store, first tannery, first blacksmith shop, and first brick house in county.

US 119/US 33, at junction with County Route 12 (Buckhannon Mountain Road), Lorentz

INDIAN BATTLE

Near here about 1790, Indians were driven back by border men under Elias Hughes. The settlements were saved by Jacob Reger, Indian fighter and scout, who ran 125 miles from Ohio River in 24 hours with warning of the savages.

Old US 33, west of Buckhannon

PRINGLE TREE

To the east (1 1/2 miles), at the mouth of Turkey Run, stood the famous Pringle Tree, so-called because in the cavity of this old sy-

The Pringle Tree near Buckhannon, Upshur County

camore, John and Samuel Pringle, who had fled from Fort Pitt, lived two years.

US 119/WV 20 near junction with County Route 119/2 (Pringle Tree Road), north of Buckhannon

HARRISON COUNTY
In 1784, Harrison County was formed from Monongalia by an Act of General Assembly. Commissioners who were to be members of the first county court met, as directed by the Assembly, at the home of George Jackson (an uncle of Stonewall Jackson) at Bush's Fort on the Buckhannon River to organize the new county. The site of the meeting is in present Upshur County, but in 1784 was a part of Harrison.

Old US 33 (Island Avenue), Buckhannon

BUCKHANNON/FRONTIER DAYS
Named for chief of Delaware Indians. John Jackson settled near in 1769. John Bush built a fort which was destroyed by Indians, 1782. A settlement which grew up there became the county seat of Harrison. W.Va. Wesleyan College is here.

To the north stood the giant tree in which Samuel and John Pringle made a home in 1764. In the Heavner Cemetery are the graves of Capt. William White, killed near the fort, and John Fink, killed near here during Indian raids.

US 119, at junction with WV 20, Buckhannon

FRENCH CREEK
Settled by colonists from New England. French Creek Academy was important early school. Asa Brooks started religious services here, 1816, from which grew the Presbyterian Church. Here, 1828, was formed early total abstinence society.

WV 20, just north of junction with County Route 32 (Slab Camp Road), French Creek

INDIAN CAMP
Indian Camp, Ash Camp, and Rock Camp were favorite camping sites of the Indians. In 1772, a party of 12 Indians, while on a peaceful hunting trip at Indian Camp, was attacked by a band of frontiersmen and not a red man escaped.

*WV 20, south of French Creek

UPSHUR MILITIA
While at drill here on Sept. 12, 1863, a company of 70 Upshur County militia under Daniel Gould was captured by a force of Confederates under Major J.K. Kesler. Seven escaped, 25 paroled, and 38 died in captivity.

WV 4, at junction with WV 20, Rock Cave

WAYNE COUNTY
Formed in 1842 from Cabell. Named for General Anthony Wayne, whose victory over the western Indians in 1794 at Fallen Timbers broke the Indian confederacy and removed the menace of the red man from western Virginia.

US 60, Wayne-Cabell border; *WV 152, Wayne-Cabell border; *WV 37, Wayne-Lincoln border; *US 52, Wayne-Mingo border; *WV 37, Wayne-Kentucky state border

VETERANS ADMINISTRATION HOSPITAL

Located one and a half mile south on Spring Valley Drive. Established, 1932, for the care and rehabilitation of American war veterans. A one hundred eighty bed General Medical and Surgical Hospital with dental and outpatient treatment.

US 60 (Waverly Road), at junction with Burlington Road, Huntington

INDIAN MOUND

A flat-topped conical burial mound in Camden Park is the largest mound in the Huntington area, and is third in size in West Virginia. It has not been excavated; was probably built by the Adena people between 1000 B.C. and A.D. 1.

US 60, Camden Park, west of Huntington

CEREDO-KENOVA

Ceredo—Founded in 1857 by Eli Thayer of Massachusetts, an Abolition leader, in his plan to create sentiment against slavery in western states. Kenova—Named for the meeting place of three states, Kentucky, Ohio, and West Virginia.

US 60, 0.1 miles east of Kenova Bridge, Kenova

WAYNE

First called Trout's Hill for Abraham Trout, who established a mill here in 1828, which ran for a century.

Entrance, Camden Park, near Huntington, W. Va.

This undated early postcard of Camden Park shows the entrance to the park, the site of the largest Native American burial mound in the Huntington area.

Large areas of this county were included in the land granted to John Savage and other veterans of the French and Indian War.

WV 152, 0.9 miles north of junction with WV 37, Wayne

REV. WAR SOLDIER'S GRAVE

Nearby is the grave of Josiah Marcum (1759-1846?). Enlisting from Bedford County, he served: In Col. Campbell's Vir. Militia Reg., 1780-81, as a wagon guard at Gen. Gates's retreat, and as a drummer at the Battle of Guilford Crt. House, NC. Early settler in Tug River Valley, a gunsmith and blacksmith, he later lived in KY and OH and was the progenitor of the area Marcum family.

*Mouth of Jennie's Creek, 1 mile south of Crum (to be erected)

FORT GAY

Named during the War between the States. At the junction of the Tug and Big Sandy rivers, in 1789, Charles Vancouver and 10 companions built a log fort and attempted a settlement on land surveyed in 1770 by John Fry for George Washington.

WV 37 (Court Street), 0.7 miles west of junction with US 52, Fort Gay

WEBSTER COUNTY

Formed, 1860, from Braxton, Nicholas and Randolph. Named for Daniel Webster. Webster County is noted for its fine mountain scenery. Its forests produced the tree that was the largest hardwood at the Chicago World's Fair, 1893.

*WV 20, Webster-Nicholas border; WV 15, Webster-Randolph border; WV 20, Webster-Upshur border

Visitors came from around the world to enjoy salt sulphur baths and springs at the Webster Springs Hotel. Completed in 1902, the hotel burned in 1926. Date unknown.

Wetzel County was named for border warfare hero Lewis Wetzel, depicted at right in a drawing by G.G. White, date unknown.

BLUE MONDAY SAND

The cliff of Webster Springs Sandstone across the highway is the "Blue Monday Sand" of the driller, which yields oil and natural gas at depths of over 1000 feet in central West Virginia.

WV 20/WV 15, Webster Springs

WEBSTER SPRINGS

Originally known as Fort Lick for salt springs, known during Revolution, which attracted herds of game. Webster Springs was important health resort for many years. Town retains name of Addison for Addison McLaughlin, owner of its site.

WV 15, courthouse square, Webster Springs

STROUD MASSACRE

The Stroud Massacre in June 1772, by the Shawnee Indians was followed by a raid upon the Delaware Indians at Bulltown by a party of enraged white men who killed every Indian there. Such incidents helped bring on Dunmore's War, 1774.

*WV 20, Camden-on-Gauley

WETZEL COUNTY

Formed in 1846 from Tyler. Named for Lewis Wetzel, the great frontiersman, who with his brothers during Indian days, ranged the settlements from their home in Marshall County throughout northern West Virginia.

173

*WV 20, Wetzel-Harrison border; US 250, Wetzel-Marion border; *WV 89, Wetzel-Marshall border; WV 2, Wetzel-Marshall border; *US 250, Wetzel-Marshall border; *WV 7, Wetzel-Monongalia border; *WV 2, Wetzel-Tyler border; WV Alternate 18, Wetzel-Tyler border*

MASON-DIXON LINE

Made famous as line between free and slave states before War Between the States. The survey establishing Maryland-Pennsylvania boundary began, 1763; halted by Indian wars, 1767; continued to southwest corner, 1782; marked, 1784.

*WV 2, Marshall-Wetzel border; *WV 69, Wetzel-Pennsylvania border*

BEFORE THE ICE AGE

Ohio Valley streams, in olden days, flowed into the Great Lakes basin. Glacial ice later blocked the path and formed a lake north of this point. The Ohio River then broke through highlands here and found an outlet to the Gulf of Mexico.

WV 2, Locust Roadside Park

NEW MARTINSVILLE

Settled by Edward Doolin who was killed here by Indians in 1785. Named for Presley Martin. Here stands a monument to Levi Morgan, a scout for the army of General St. Clair. He was a noted Indian fighter who killed 100 red men.

WV 2 and WV 20, New Martinsville

VAN CAMP

Village settled early 1800s, named for pioneer Steven (1793-1873) and family in 1840s. John and Margaret Van Camp gave land for Methodist E. Church, 1879; services held into 1940s; cemetery dates to 1851; site for school, ca. 1870-1920, given by family; post office & general store served the community. Clarksburg Northern Railroad provided access to village until early 20th century.

WV 180, Van Camp

HUNDRED

Henry Church, who died in 1860 at the age of 109, was familiarly known as "Old Hundred" and the town was named for him. He was a soldier in the British Army under Cornwallis and was captured by American troops under Gen. Lafayette.

US 250, at junction with WV 69, Hundred

WIRT COUNTY

Formed, 1848, from Wood and Jackson. Named for William Wirt, who was prominent in the prosecution of Aaron Burr. Development of the Burning Springs oil fields started in 1859, year of the Titusville, Pennsylvania oil boom.

*WV 5, Wirt-Calhoun border; County Route 21, Wirt-Jackson border; *WV 47, Wirt-Ritchie border; *WV 53, Wirt-Ritchie border; *WV 14, Wirt-Roane border; *WV 47, Wirt-Wood border; *WV 14, Wirt-Wood border; *County Route 21, Wirt-Wood border*

BURNING SPRINGS SAND

The Freeport Sandstone, the "Burning Springs Sand" of the driller, is brought to the surface in the quarry by the sharp upwarp of Burning Springs (Volcano) Anticline. This sandstone yields oil to wells on the hills above and seeps oil in the quarry.

WV 47, near Cisco

WELLS LOCK AND DAM NO. 3

Built 1867-74 by Kanawha Navigation Company at cost of $60,000. Dam is 289 ft. long with 42 ft. wide base anchored to bedrock. Lockchamber is 22 ft. wide and 125 ft. long with a 11.8 ft. lift. Purchased by Federal Government, 1905, and partially rebuilt, 1908. Federal operation of project for commercial navigation on Little Kanawha River ended 1951.

1 mile from junction of WV 14 and 14/7, north of Elizabeth

ELIZABETH

Settled by William Beauchamp, 1796. Named for wife of David Beauchamp. Near here in 1752, Christopher Gist placed a marker for the Ohio Company, whose plan to colonize the western lands was halted by the French and Indian War.

Junction of Washington and Court streets, courthouse square, Elizabeth

RUBLE CHURCH

One of the oldest "still attended" churches in the state, it was built in 1835 of hand-hewed logs. Much effort has been expended on the preservation of church's original appearance. It is heated by a pot-bellied stove and lighted by kerosene lights. Deed book states that all denominations, except those of "Northern Principles," were welcome. Many graves in the church cemetery predate the Civil War.

WV 5, at junction with County Route 35/6 (Chestnut Road), southeast of Elizabeth

RATHBONE WELL

The first well in West Virginia drilled solely for petroleum was located near the mouth of Burning Springs Run. The well was drilled with a "spring pole" by the Rathbones and others from Parkersburg, begun in 1859, completed May, 1860. Produced at the rate of 100 barrels per day. In 1863 General Jones commanding Confederate forces set fire to the oil stored in tanks, barrels and boats, destroying in a day an estimated 300,000 barrels of oil.

WV 5, Burning Springs

Rathbone Well at Burning Springs, begun in 1859, was the first petroleum well in the state. This photo shows an oil field at Burning Springs, circa 1900.

POPULATION CENTER

The population center of the United States was in present West Virginia four times as it moved westward across the nation: near Wardensville in 1820; at Smoke Hole in 1830; west of Buckhannon in 1840; near Burning Springs in 1850.

WV 5, Burning Springs

WOOD COUNTY

Formed in 1798 from Kanawha and Harrison. Named for James Wood, governor of Virginia. Blennerhassett Island, scene of the Burr-Blennerhassett plot to establish a colony in southwestern territory, is important historic landmark.

*WV 68, Wood-Jackson border; *WV 2, Wood-Pleasants border; *US 50, Wood-Ritchie border; *County Route 21, Wood-Wirt border; *WV 14, Wood-Wirt border;*

US 50, Wood-Ohio state border; WV 14, Williamstown, Wood-Ohio state border

DUNMORE'S CAMP

Lord Dunmore's army train camped here in 1774 on the way into the Indian country. The route followed the old trail, crossing the Ohio at the mouth of Hocking River. Here in 1791 Indians killed Nicholas Carpenter and party.

WV 2, Waverly

TOMLINSON MANSION

This restored colonial brick mansion built, 1839, by Joseph Tomlinson III, is town's oldest home. John Audubon, famous U.S. naturalist who painted and wrote about birds of North America, spent some time here studying birds of the area.

WV 14 (Highland Avenue), at junction with Poplar Avenue, Williamstown

1859 view of Parkersburg showing the junction of the Little Kanawha and Ohio Rivers

177

WILLIAMSTOWN

Named for Isaac Williams, who settled here in 1787 on land pre-empted in 1770 by Joseph Tomlinson and his children, Joseph, Samuel, and Rebecca. Williams, veteran of border wars, married Rebecca. Court met at their home in 1800.

WV 14 (Highland Avenue), in park, Williamstown

PARKERSBURG

Blockhouse at "Point" built by Virginia for border defense during Indian hostilities. Garrisoned by troops under Bogard, Coburn, and others. Still standing in 1803. County seat established in 1800 on land given by John Stokeley.

WV 14/WV 68, Federal Building, Parkersburg

West Virginia's first governor, Arthur I. Boreman of Parkersburg, circa 1870

WEST VIRGINIA'S FIRST GOVERNOR/ PARKERSBURG GOVERNORS

Arthur I. Boreman presided at June 1861 Wheeling Convention where statehood plan formulated. Elected state's first governor June 20, 1863, he served three, two-year terms, resigning in 1869 to take U.S. Senate seat. Parkersburg attorney served as Wood County Circuit Judge 1861-1863 and 1888-1896. He is buried in Parkersburg Memorial Gardens.

Parkersburg was home for four of West Virginia's first 11 governors. Arthur I. Boreman (1823-96), first governor, served 1863-69; W.E. Stevenson (1820-83), third governor, served 1869-71; Jacob B. Jackson (1829-93), sixth governor, served 1881-85; A.B. White (1856-1941), eleventh governor, served 1901-05.

Corner of 3rd and Market streets (behind the Wood County Courthouse), Parkersburg

OLD TURNPIKES

Washington, who had favored the Braddock Road, proposed the Northwestern Turnpike to the Ohio through Virginia in 1784. It was completed to Parkersburg in 1838. The road from Staunton to Parkersburg was opened in 1847.

*US 50/WV 47, Parkersburg

OLD TOLLGATE HOUSE

Here is the site of the Old Tollgate House where the Staunton-Parkersburg Turnpike and the Northwestern Turnpike met. Surveyed by Col. Claudius Crozet, both roads were completed to the Ohio River by 1850.

US 50/WV 47, Parkersburg

NEAL'S STATION

Neal's Station or Fort Neal was built in 1785 by Capt. James Neal, Revolutionary War veteran, who led a party of settlers to the mouth of the Little Kanawha. Neal first came here in 1783 surveying present site of Parkersburg.

WV 95 (Camden Avenue), at junction with East Street, Parkersburg

COL. HUGH PHELPS

Wood County formally organized, August 12, 1799, at the home of Colonel Hugh Phelps, who came here, 1787. Phelps made the first effort to arrest Burr and Blennerhassett. About 1800, he built this house, later the home of Thomas Tavenner.

WV 95 (Camden Avenue), at junction with East Street, Parkersburg

GEORGE ROGERS CLARK

At the Little Kanawha, 1774, George Rogers Clark and 90 companions, largely recruited in what is now West Virginia, assembled on their way into Kentucky. Their plans, halted by Indian wars, later resulted in conquest of the Northwest.

Blennerhassett boat dock in Point Park, Parkersburg

Harman Blennerhassett, 1796

PREHISTORIC SITES

In addition to its historic importance, Blennerhassett Island also contains important prehistoric sites. Several Indian villages exist on the Island, and large collections of Indian artifacts have been found here. Largest of the sites, a Fort Ancient village, has now been washed away by the Ohio River, but smaller ones still remain. Artifacts found on the Island indicate occupation dating from 10,000 years ago.

WV 68, at junction with WV 95, 3 miles southwest of Parkersburg

BURR-BLENNERHASSETT

Harman Blennerhassett purchased island in 1797, and built for his bride a mansion which became the showplace of the Ohio Valley. Aaron Burr was his guest in 1805. Here they planned a military expedition with the intention to conquer the Southwest.

*County Route 30, 0.8 miles from junction with WV 892

WASHINGTON BOTTOM

A tract of 2314 acres acquired by

George Washington three miles west on December 15, 1772, for services in the French and Indian War. It was surveyed by William Crawford in June, 1771. It bordered for five miles on the Ohio River.

WV 892, at Washington Community Building, Washington

BELLEVILLE

Just north of here, Joseph Wood built a fort in 1785 on land first patented by Dr. James Craik, friend of Geo. Washington. Garrisoned by Virginia troops in 1791, it was the most important outpost between the Kanawha and Little Kanawha rivers.

WV 68, just north of junction with County Route 17 (Lee Creek Road), Belleville

MORGAN'S RAIDERS

At Buffington's Island below Belleville, July, 1863, General John H. Morgan's noted Confederate cavalrymen were defeated. In their flight, some of his men passed this point en route into Virginia. General Morgan and many men were captured in Ohio.

*WV 14, at junction with County Route 21, Mineral Wells

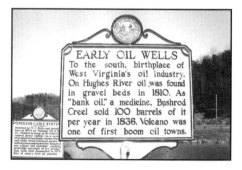

EARLY OIL WELLS

To the south, birthplace of West Virginia's oil industry. On Hughes River oil was found in gravel beds in 1810. As "bank oil," a medicine, Bushrod Creel sold 100 barrels of it per year in 1836. Volcano was one of first boom oil towns.

County Route 5, 3 miles north of Volcano

ENDLESS CABLE SYSTEM

Invented by W.C. Stiles and installed here in 1870's by Volcanic Oil & Gas Co. Pumped as many as 40 wells from central power station via a system of graduated handmade wooden wheels and cables which conveyed motion to walking beam and sucker rod. Required one engine and operator, enabling profitable operation of low production wells until dismantled in 1979. Site of state's first oil pipeline.

County Route 5, 3 miles north of Volcano

WYOMING COUNTY

Formed in 1850 from Logan. Named for the Wyoming tribe of Indians. First settler was John Cooke; first permanent settlement, Oceana. County has vast areas of smokeless coal. Among its natural features is Castle Rock.

*WV 85, Wyoming-Boone border; WV 10, Wyoming-Logan border; *WV 16, Wyoming-McDowell border; *US 52/WV 80, Wyoming-McDowell border; *WV 10, Wyoming-Mercer border; *US 52, Wyoming-Mingo border; *WV 54, Wyoming-Raleigh border; WV 16,

Wyoming-Raleigh border; *WV 99, Wyoming-Raleigh border

PREHISTORIC PETROGLYPHS

Nearby are ancient rock carvings of unknown age or purpose. Some think early Celtic explorers carved them. Others believe Native Americans more likely carved them prior to 1000 AD.

WV 971, south of Oceana; WV 10, near Logan-Wyoming border

JOHN COOKE

First settler of Wyoming County. He was born in London, 1752, and kidnaped and sold to Virginia planter as an indenture servant. He was a revolutionary soldier, and fought in battles of Point Pleasant, Monmouth and Stony Point. In lieu of army pay, he was given grant of land in Montgomery County, Virginia, located on "Little Laurel", on which he and two sons settled, 1799. He is buried here in the Delilah Chapel graveyard.

WV 10, 0.3 miles east of junction with WV 85, Laurel Park, Oceana

PINEVILLE

Here is the statue of Rev. W.H. Cook, soldier, statesman, and minister. Oceana was the county seat for many years. Wyoming County is noted for the Burning Rocks where warm air from the earth's depths melt ice or snow in winter.

WV 10, at junction with WV 97 (Main Avenue), courthouse square, Pineville

This temporary Wyoming County Courthouse in Pineville, 1911, was replaced by the current courthouse in 1916.

ITMANN

Pocahontas Fuel Co. coal mining town, 1916, named for Isaac T. Mann, Pres. Italian stonemasons built large Co. store/office bldg., 1923-25 on plans of Alex Mahood, a noted WV architect. Placed on National Register in 1990. Ritter Lumber Co. shipped 200 ready-made company houses on N&W and Virginian and erected here. Mine's 125,000 tons in 1919 led county, closed 1928-49; operated again until 1986.

WV 16, Itmann

MULLENS

Settled by A.J. Mullins, 1894. Change in spelling by failure to dot "i". Center of Smokeless coal field.

First commercial coal mine in this county was opened here in 1908. The Virginian Railroad reached the town, 1906. Incorporated, 1912.

Moran Avenue and 4th Street, two blocks north of junction with WV 16, Mullens

Mullens, date unknown

Index

Entries in all capital letters and aligned left denote marker titles

187

188

203

Z

Photo Credits

The historic photographs used in this publication are from the West Virginia State Archives, including the following special collections:

Beckley Exhibition Coal Mine Collection
William Blizzard Collection
Boyd Blynn Stutler Collection
Camp Washington-Carver Collection
Department of Natural Resources Collection
Joseph H. Diss Debar Collection
Elkem Metals Collection
William Forbes Collection
Grant's Photo Record
John Edward Kenna Collection
Meadow River Lumber Company Collection
Robert R. Keller Collection
West Virginia Coal Life Project
West Virginia Geological Survey
William W. Smith Collection